HappyDays

HappyDays
The Life & Times of a Short Session Carp Angler

CHRIS HASWELL

Edited & designed by Mike Starkey

Published by
FishingBookSender

First published by FishingBookSender, 2012

For ordering information contact:
Fishingbooksender,
Caerbannog, Sarn, Powys SY16 4EX
Telephone 05601 972040
email: info@fishingbooksender.co.uk
www.fishingbooksender.com

ISBN 978-0-9574283-1-7

Contents

Acknowledgements

I would like to dedicate this book to my mother, Constance Irene Haswell, who worked her socks off doing God knows how many hours a week to bring up three kids on her own whilst earning a pittance as a nurse. She always seemed to know when it was the right time to send a cab up to Keston to bring me home such as when it was freezing cold or pouring with rain.

To my kids, George, Harry, Freddie, and Carmella, of whom I am immensely proud and I love to bits.

To Ken Rowley and the late Steve Edwards who taught me to carp fish and put up with me through my wild years during the seventies, (not a pretty story), and who became lifelong friends.

To Tony Tappenden for writing a Preface and who I have fished with for as long as I can remember. He is a true and very dear friend and constant source of amusement and entertainment and he is not a bad angler either. I have to say that or he would thump me!

And to all those friends I have met along the way (far too many to mention here) that have made the last forty-seven years an eye opener, and a never-to-be-forgotten experience, even if some of those experiences would be better off forgotten!

My thanks to Lee Jackson for writing the Foreword. I have known Lee since the seventies and he has always been the same person, despite being the ex British Carp Record Holder, and now the World Champion carp guru. To which after consuming six bottles of red wine recently he reminded me no less than twenty-seven times, "Did you know I am a World Champion?" Lee remains level headed, helpful and modest, well except when he is on the sauce!

To Jerry Thornton-Jones for his excellent painting for the bookjacket and the drawing of Keston. Tim Paisley for finding some lost photographs. Fred Wilton for letting me use his emails and of course for inspiring me and helping me learn about bait.

Oh, and Dave and Mike for putting up with my ramblings and my incredible lack of diction and spelling . . . particularly Mike who has done his utmost to allow me to write this book in my own words even though he must have thought at times, "What is this bloke on?"

See you when the sun rises! Oh HAPPY DAYS indeed . . . **Chris (HAPPY) Haswell**

Editor's Note: Many of the photographs in this book have been reproduced from 35mm transparencies. A number of them showed signs of water damage in that they were covered all over in small black dots. They were passed through software that elimated much of the dust, scratches and imperfections but some still show evidence of the marks. The decision was to use them as they were an essential part of the story.

Lee Jackson

I can remember being at a rehearsal studio on Canvey Island in Essex, my head tilted backwards toward the PA speaker to enable me to properly hear the notes that were expertly being emitted from my bass guitar, and then looking across at the guy holding the microphone, waiting for him to start singing. And then he did, which immediately caused me to lose concentration and play a few bum notes as I just couldn't believe such a beautiful sound could come out of something so ugly! After a while I settled back into the rhythm of things, closed my eyes and then imagined myself being part of the backing band at a Bryan Adams concert, boy, could this bloke sing. This bloke was Chris Haswell, a friend that I had known for years, and although I was told he could sing a bit, I never imagined he'd be as good as what he was and still is.

In all probability I had first seen Chris as far back as the mid 1960s when I was fishing down at Keston Ponds for absolutely anything that came along, because occasionally I'd see these mysterious looking characters turn up, all wearing drab clothing and floppy hats, and quietly going about the task of catching the equally as mysterious carp. I can remember thinking to myself that one day I'd like to have a go at catching one of those, trouble was at this stage in my life all the floppy hats were far too big!

A few years later and I was a carp angler proper, well at least I had all the gear, although no idea. It was the start of the season and I was fishing The Ballast Pit in Tonbridge, struggling to catch as per usual, when all of a sudden three very familiar mysterious looking characters went walking down the far bank, got themselves set up, and immediately started catching carp. I was quite pleased that my floppy hat was still a bit big for me, as it meant that I could pull it down over my eyes and ears so that I didn't have to bear the torture and embarrassment of seeing or hearing these anglers catching carp after carp after carp whilst I was failing miserably. Later in life I recognised these three anglers as Steve Edwards, Ken Rowley and of course Chris, consistently catching carp back then and consistently catching them for years to follow.

Out of the three of them Chris was the one that I came to know the most, often bumping into him on various waters around Kent, and getting into conversations with him about this, that and the other and usually finishing up on a subject that we both had a common interest in, which was bait. There was one occasion when I bumped, or rather stumbled, upon him fishing a water down at Sevenoaks, stumbling upon him being an understatement because I almost couldn't see him due to everything being camouflaged. I couldn't believe it, everything, rods, reels, bite alarms, landing net pole and arms, bivvy, clothing; everything had been meticulously painted and disguised to blend in with the surroundings. I must admit I did take the micky out of him a bit, but although I could never have had admitted it at the time, deep down I thought that it all looked really smart. Well, although he couldn't be seen by day, when it got dark, and people that knew him back then will know what I'm about to say, by complete contrast, at night his entire swim would light up like Blackpool Illuminations! Honestly, if you had walked into his swim with a Geiger counter it would've blown a fuse, there were isotopes absolutely everywhere. I remember fishing on the opposite bank to him one night and sort of hoping that we weren't on the flight path to Gatwick, it must've been ever so confusing for airline pilots; I imagined that any minute he'd have a Boeing 747 land in his swim! I don't know if he knows this, but because of his passion for isotopes, for a while he acquired the nickname of 'Dizzy Chernobyl', which had something to do with the catastrophic nuclear accident that lit up and contaminated almost the entire Soviet Union.

The nickname I prefer for him however is 'Happy', a nickname that accurately sums this man up, as rarely, other than when he has to put his hand in his pocket to splash out on fishing tackle, does he ever not have a smile on his face. There are a couple of other nicknames he has acquired over the years, 'Mr Angry' and 'Poison Pen' due to him writing the odd magazine article that has upset a few people, but such is life, you can't please everybody all of the time when you speak your mind and put your thoughts into words.

I felt quite honoured to have been asked to write this foreword for Chris as there are a million others that he could have asked, I suppose it sort of reflects the mutual respect that we have for each other. Like me, Chris has been carp fishing for many years, forty-two years in my case and something like half a century in his. In that time we have seen it all, been there, done it, got the T-shirts and seen all the changes. One thing that doesn't change however is that deep down burning desire to fish for carp, I was going to say catch carp but that's not what it's all about. Everything about carp fishing is special in its own way, the preparation, the bait and rig formulation, being at one with nature, having a bit of a laugh with friends, the extreme excitement, adrenalin rush and urgency of a bite, the awesome beauty of some of the carp that are caught and the unconscious dreams of the mysterious monster that might be next to succumb to the bait.

I'm really looking forward to reading this book, the book of a friend and somebody that I respect as a person, for his angling ability and as a fishing acquaintance. I bump into Chris quite regularly now as we are both fishing on the same water, and you know what, he's got older but hasn't changed, has still got a smile on his face and I can imagine him walking along the far bank with that old floppy hat on, on his way to catching even more carp.

Carp fishing is like a drug, it gets a hold on you, often rules your life and sometimes ruins your mind - "Arrest him officer, he's been indulging in drugs for over fifty years."

Happy Days indeed . . . Enjoy
Lee

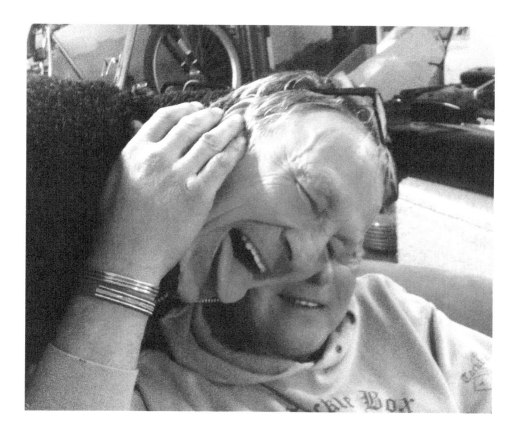

Tony Tappenden

'Happy and Tappy' - as we are known

Chris and I have been fishing together now for many years and we have fished stacks of waters together, especially in Kent. I can honestly say we have enjoyed every minute and at times it has been hard, but hey that is carp fishing for you especially within the carp fraternity. There is so much competition between one another and this is long before you even start fishing!

For me personally I found that the Leisure Sport Sutton water was my most trying time in my fishing times and feel that it was and still is, one of the hardest waters in Kent. If you have fished Sutton, as Happy and I have many times, you will know what I am talking about The size of the fish in there far outweighs, the hard times but all it needs is one capture like for myself when I caught Blind Eye at 42lb8oz – that makes everything worthwhile.

Chris and I have met some great friends and had some good times down there and laughs especially when I took up body piercing. Chris will remember me piercing his nose after him smelling my brolly - the only regret I have is that we should have taken pictures of it. I have loads of stories about Chris (and me) over the years and could go on forever, but as a best mate and a fishing partner I think we have made a good team. BUT he's a lot older than me ha, ha, and he can sing a bit!!

All the best mate, Tappy

For as long as I can remember I have enjoyed fishing, most of my friends I grew up with on Bromley common went fishing, probably because we had no money to do anything else. Fishing is undoubtedly a form of escapism. Maybe we were all escaping from the trappings of the council estate we all grew up on, maybe it allowed us to have a bit of freedom and time out together exploring the big new world around us. I don't know, but whatever the reason, fishing had got into my blood. Once I had spent time learning to fish for most species I ended up becoming intrigued by how majestic carp appeared to be, like the Kings of the lake, for want of a better word. Ever since those early days I have had a passion for carp fishing. For some, carp fishing is a way of life, but for me personally it has always been what it is, a pastime. Like most people my carp fishing has had to be a weekend interest as apart from when I fished Redmire Pool I have had to fit my fishing into weekends. This was fine years ago when there really were not that many carp anglers around, but it is a bit different nowadays. Carp anglers are everywhere and have been for the last twenty to twenty-five years. The popularity of carp fishing has escalated to epic proportions. There can be no doubt that trying to fish weekends on most waters is now a very difficult situation. That's why I am more sympathetic towards the short session angler than those who are fortunate enough to sit on the lake all week, for surely the two are worlds apart. I know all about the sacrifices that long term anglers are supposed to make in order to fish all week, but I just can't relate to it. That kind of fishing is way over my head and not relevant to anything I do. That is not meant as a criticism but an observation. Although things have changed slightly in the last few years and I can now get down the lake midweek. I have now at the time of writing this book been carp fishing for forty-seven years, so I guess you could say I've done a bit. I would consider myself OLD SCHOOL, something I consider an advantage rather than a hindrance. In fact only recently I was talking to Martin Locke and he came out with a great saying, "There's no school like the old school!" How true is that? For over twenty years I have written for monthly carp fishing magazines and contributed chapters in carp fishing books. I ran my own bait company for well over twenty-five years and also ran the Kent region of the British Carp Study Group (BCSG) for a few years. I joined it as a fresh faced seventeen-year-old way back in 1970 - a year after the BCSG was founded, possibly making me the youngest ever person to join the BCSG. Back then The BCSG held most of the best carp anglers in the country within its membership. I have to say I felt like an imposter as I had to join in order to fish Ashlea Pool, which I also did in 1970 with my lifelong friend Ken Rowley.

I have fished countless waters in my time but mostly in Kent. Outside of Kent, if my memory serves me well, I have fished Yateley, Horton, Ashlea Pool, Redmire Pool, Crayfish Pool, Wraysbury, Orchid, Dorchester Lagoon, Pippingford Park and Tooting Common. There are loads of other waters I have fished but I have no memory of them. There are one or two I shouldn't have gone to. Apart from Redmire, I never did that much time on any of the aforementioned waters as it soon became obvious that in order to approach most of the waters I mentioned you needed far more time than I had at my disposal. I think I am a realist in that for most of my time in carp fishing I have fished on Saturday nights. In order to form any kind of plan or campaign I have had to fish within an hour's drive or less from where I have lived in order to keep in touch with my chosen water. It is slightly different now, however, as I live in an area which has an abundance of lakes with a wealth of very big carp within twenty minutes of my home. As my old mate Tony Tappenden says . . . "Why drive past lakes that hold massive carp to fish somewhere else an hour or two's drive away?" Most of the lakes in the area are difficult, pressured waters, but isn't that what makes us do it?

I have never really thought about writing a book until recently when I was asked to write a chapter in *It's A Long Old Road*, a book dedicated to my lifelong friend Steve Edwards, who sadly died of cancer in 2010. It was a fitting tribute to Steve written by long time friends and the odd acquaintance. The publisher, Dave Griffiths, and editor & designer Mike Starkey, had very kindly offered to wave their fees so the proceeds of sales of the book could be donated to the Macmillan Cancer Trust. To cut a long story short, Dave and Mike liked my style of writing so very kindly offered me the chance to write this book. It is my intention to write this book with as much truth as is possible to mention without incriminating myself, also with as much humour as is legally possible and with as much honesty without giving the game away too much. To be perfectly honest I was struggling to come up with a title and it was my old mate Tony's suggestion to call the book 'HAPPY DAYS', as my nickname has been HAPPY for as long as I can remember. There are those who think my name is Happy because I am a miserable so and so, but as usual they are people who haven't got a clue what I am like, nor do they know me. It may have been Steve Edwards who first called me Happy, I cant remember now but Happy Days probably reflects my carp fishing far more than my idea of a title . . . *Confessions of a Part Time Angler* . . . That title would have been more appropriate for a soft porn film during the seventies I think! As you work your way through the book I hope you pick up on the fact that I like my carp fishing with good friends, good company and a sense of humour. Of course there are moments of seriousness but they are reserved for times when seriousness is required and usually reserved for when it's time to buy another round! Above all Happy Days is a reflection of forty-seven year's worth of short session fishing, accounts, humour and findings along the way, even if somewhat confrontational at times. I have always spoken my mind, which has got me in trouble over the years, but isn't that what makes life interesting? How dull would life be if we were all the same? In my humble opinion there are far too many people who take themselves far too seriously in carp fishing these days, it's only bloody carp fishing lads! I have been very privileged to have met and formed friendships with some of the country's best and most pioneering carp anglers of my generation and have learned so much from them. That knowledge and those friendships I value immensely. Oh, and one last thing, if you hope to discover the meaning of life within these pages, or hope to look at countless pictures of huge carp, then you may be better off buying some one else's book . . .

Chapter One

Caesar's Pool -
The Beginning

I first started carp fishing way back in the season of 1964/5, and used to cycle the five miles or so up to Keston Fishponds. Occasionally I would even walk it from my home on Bromley Common.

The ponds were later named Caesar's Pool, and also the well that feeds the River Ravensbourne is called Caesar's Well, mainly because of the history and legend that surrounds the area. There are Roman and Iron Age burial sites dating back to 3000bc and the ponds are fed by natural underground springs. I believe the ponds were built between 1823 and c1827 by John Ward, a wealthy merchant, to form a reservoir from which water was pumped to his house for fresh water. The pool was used by the Keston swimming club before the First World War, and amazingly the crazy buggers used to dive in for a swim on New Year's day. There were two diving boards, one on each side of the pool, built right on the edge of the shelf where the deep water starts. The remnants of these can still be seen today in the form of six inch solid oak posts which protrude up from the water.

I have no idea when the lakes were first stocked with coarse fish, I do know however, that there has always been an abundance of roach, rudd, perch, tench, eels and pike. There seems to be reports of carp being introduced, I believe, in the early to mid 1930s and again in the late 1950s, with a few fish from Summerhill near Tonbridge. All of the carp were of the Leney strain. More were stocked at a much later date by Thames Water.

I had been fishing the ponds for the roach, rudd, and tench that were, as usual, the main target for us as kids. At the time I first started fishing there were just the original carp before the Thames Water stocking. As I said earlier, I used to fish for the other species in the pool which was pretty standard back then and amongst the fish I caught some cracking sized tench. Most anglers that started to fish for carp did so after they had become accomplished at fishing for other coarse fish - pretty much like doing an apprenticeship. It was while general coarse fishing that I started to notice these huge black-backed scaly monsters that would rise up through the early morning mist and hang momentarily before crashing back into the inky black depths of the pool, sending huge ripples out across the surface. Coots and moorhens would shriek in protest at the interruption of their early morning feeding session.

There was at that time an old boy called Ron who also fished the ponds. He was a master angler and would cycle up to the ponds from Coney Hall on his old Raleigh bicycle with his rods, keep net, landing net and umbrella tied to his crossbar with old shoelaces. Ron would always catch more and bigger specimens than anyone

Two photos of Keston Pond circa 1960 (Frith Collection)

else. The memory of those days lingers in my mind like it was yesterday. The only sound you would hear across the tranquil pool would be the sound of Ron's old transistor radio pumping out songs of the sixties . . . "Grocer jack, grocer jack get off your back, go into town, don't let them down, oh no, no . . ." a classic song of the time! As the memories flood back into my mind so does the smell of maggots - that overpowering aroma of ammonia which accompanied the purchase of gentles. God, how I miss those days. One morning I was talking to Ron as he wound in yet another pound and a half rudd when a huge fish crashed out of the water in front of the railings where we were fishing. I couldn't believe the power of the fish. "What the hell was that, Ron?" I asked. "That, my son, was a carp - an almost mythical fish. I have been fishing here for years son, and I have never seen one landed nor seen anyone get a bite from one of them." We watched in amazement as the two square yard area of bubbles hit the surface of the pool like a cauldron of froth and out came the fish again. A huge head and shoulders that shook from side to side like a demented whale before crashing back into the pool. You could see almost every single scale along the fish's flank which shone like gold medallions in the early morning sunshine. That was it, I was hooked and that day became the first day of my lifetime pursuit of fishing for carp.

Caesar's Pool was to be the start of my carp fishing apprenticeship. As time went by I acquired better fishing tackle - an eight foot tank aerial was my first serious rod coupled with an old centre pin reel. Now I was equipped to take on the elusive Caesar's Pool carp. Somewhere around this time I became aware of a couple of strange looking characters that fished the pool. They both wore odd attire, dark, shabby clothes, floppy hats and their rods, reels and bank sticks were all painted matt black. They would blend into their surroundings, sit motionless hour after hour and the only time they would break the trend would be to quietly tiptoe up to the other one for a few words before returning to their rods. I just had to meet these two as they could possibly help in my quest to learn more about these fish called carp. One evening, after fishing for the day, I decided to wander round the pool to introduce myself to them. I approached the first one, feeling so out of place in my lime green Sloppy Joe jumper and as the words, "Hello mate," started to escape from my mouth the immortal words . . . "F*** off!" reverberated in my ears. I was completely stunned. With a wave of his hand the bloke just gestured that I should keep on walking. Now I was really apprehensive as to whether the second bloke would be so abrasive. I approached him and said, "Hello mate, you caught anything?" It was a huge relief when he said, "No mate, not yet." Over the next couple of hours the bloke did his very best to answer all of my 500 questions a minute. It transpired that they were none other than Steve Edwards and Ken Rowley - noted carp anglers of the day. They took me under their wings and very generously taught me everything they had learned over the previous few years they had been carp fishing. It was Steve who had been somewhat caustic when we had first met but soon as he realised that I was deadly serious about fishing for carp he, like Ken, gave me all the help he could.

I've met some real characters while fishing the Pool. One of Steve's closest friends was a guy called Terry Davey. Steve called him 'Terry the Mad', with good reason as the geezer used to smoke very big roll ups (well it was the sixties man) and used to take a stuffed dog fishing with him. That dog always had a college scarf tied round its neck. Terry would sit it up in the branches of the nearest tree and hold a conversation with it for hours . . . in fact I think Terry spent more time talking to the stuffed dog than he did fishing and he used to attract some strange looks from the local dog walkers. Let's face it, when was the last time you saw a geezer up a tree having a conversation with a stuffed dog? Those early days were magical. Like the Three Musketeers we would spend countless hours trying to fathom out what made these carp so hard to catch. We would sit up trees for hours on end watching these huge fish bury their heads deep into the black, oozing lake bed while sending up dense clouds of muddy silt and frothy bubbles. Time and time again we would lower our bread flake into the path of these fish, shaking in anticipation of a bite or a pull of the line but it never came. What did we have to do in order to hook one of these elusive creatures? As time went by we started to think along the lines of using something more natural - something closer to their natural diet. We used to go out at night with a torch after it had rained and you could clearly see lobworms all over the lawn in the torch beam. I used to use my mum's white cotton gloves to pick the worms up so they couldn't slip through my fingers but she was never too pleased to find her best cotton gloves covered in worm slime and tossed on the table. As time went by we noticed that after a heavy rainfall, the water ran down the steep banks and into the pool. Within a couple of hours the margins became very clouded and the carp would then slowly make their way into the clouded areas to feed. If you looked very carefully, you could just make out the shapes of the carp as they glided slowly along the marginal shelf. Obviously the carp felt more confident when the margins were all clouded up and our new natural bait of lobworm would be cast free lined into the path of an oncoming fish. I can vividly remember my heart pounding against my rib cage and my whole body shaking as tails of carp, feeding slowly, waved over the spot where my bait lay. All of a sudden the line pulled up and cut through the water and a huge eruption exploded. As I lifted the tank aerial into the air and pulled into an angry Caesar's Pool carp it began to do its best to plough through the dense lilies to put as much distance between us as possible. The centre-pin reel burned my fingers as I tried to slow down the carp on its journey - everything creaked as the 8lb line took its toll on the carp and slowed it down to a dead stop. When the carp boiled on the surface, a flash of scales revealed the fish to be a common carp. Slowly but surely I coaxed the carp back into the margins. How I managed to ease it back through the dense lilies without getting snagged up in the dense roots I will never know. The carp wallowed over and over as I drew it back towards the waiting landing net and with one last thrash of its tail it was in the net. At last I had landed a Caesar's Pool carp after almost two long years of trying to catch one of the residents of this super hard pool. I stood knee deep in the waterfall and after removing the hook I weighed the fish on my 25lb Salter scales and it went just over 10lb - a double figured carp. My very first carp and a Caesar's Pool carp. At last I was a genuine carp angler, the year was 1967 and it was 16th June. Both Steve and Ken wholeheartedly congratulated me. Finally I felt a great sense of relief and pride that I had stuck it out and persevered. The next time I saw old Ron I said to him, "I've cracked it Ron and caught a Keston carp." He too, was really genuinely pleased for me. I think I gained his respect that day. That was the first of many carp from Keston during my time there. My biggest regret is that in those days we just could not afford a camera and I believe I only have a handful of pictures of carp before 1970. The few I have were taken by other people, but the things that can never be erased are memories.

As we moved towards the late sixties we started to watch anglers who would fish along the railings that prevented cars from accidently going into the pool. The dam wall is actually Fishponds Road - a 'rat run' that at night can become quite busy. During the day the railings would have as many as fifteen or more anglers along it, all piling in maggots, groundbait, mashed up bread and all manner of food items. Once it got dark the dam would be deserted as you took your life in your hands if you fished at night along the railings. While we were fishing other swims around the pool, at night, we would listen to the carp crashing all along the railings, obviously having a major free feed up on all the food items that had been thrown in during the day. At that time I think it was Ken who had managed to locate a maggot farm over on the far side of St Mary Cray - the Cray Bait Farm. We started to buy gallons of huge maggots off this bloke for, I think a price of £3 or £5 pounds a gallon. There was something about his maggots that struck us because usually breeders of maggots bred them over old meat, but he was breeding his over fish offal. His were by far the biggest, the best and the smelliest. I have had a

Keston in 1968, a 16lb mirror

recent conversation with Ken on the subject and we agreed that without a doubt those maggots gave us an edge. Could it have been that the maggots had a fishy flavour and the carp were able to detect this? It makes you wonder. By now we had started fishing with floats and the lift method with a shot or two four inches from the hook in size 16 with a couple of maggots on it. We used to make our own floats in those days out of goose quills that were bright white. We would cut them up into six inch lengths and slip a bicycle valve rubber over one end and thread the line through that so the float wouldn't slip up the line. At night we would use a great big torch that had a square battery that screwed onto it with two nuts a bit like wing nuts. They held the battery onto the terminals of the torch. The torch was placed just higher than the surface of the water on a biscuit tin and it lit up a runway of light across to the far side of the lake. In those days we were the only ones crazy enough to fish all night so the light wouldn't be in any one's eyes on the far bank. The white floats stood out like tall white towers in the light of the beam. To be perfectly honest, if I could get away with using a dirty great big torch shining across the lake at night these days, I would fish that method today. It is complete nonsense to suggest that bright lights scare carp. Many times I have heard other anglers say, "Look at that idiot with the bright head-torch over there." I tend to have an inner chuckle thinking just how bright our torches used to be and the fact that carp become accustomed to their surroundings very quickly. I am sure that if you wave a torch about all over the place, they may well spook but if that beam of light is concentrated across the surface and doesn't move and you have a gallon or two of maggots spread over the margins, then I think you may well find that the carp will definitely not be put off by the light. We always used to put the light on prior to it getting dark so should any carp turn up over the baited area, then they got used to the light. It is an awesome way of fishing with two floats side by side, maybe two to three feet apart. You see every bubble, every swirl of the float, as it gently sways back and forth when a carp's tail brushes the line, feeding greedily on the maggots on the lake bed. When a carp takes the bait, the float spins in a circle, bobs and then lifts right up out of the water before tearing off under the surface. Up goes the rod and off goes the carp. Give me that kind of fishing any day compared to sitting watching motionless indicators. Back in those days we used to take our lives in our hands by sitting at night along the railings, torches on, sprung chairs to sit on and umbrellas tied to the upright, concrete posts. We surely were insane in view of the cars speeding by during the night. The worst times were after rain when the puddles used to extend halfway across the road and the drivers thought it was great fun to speed through the puddles at night and absolutely soak us as we sat focused on the floats in the beam of the torch. Ha, ha, ha - yes, we were definitely off our trolleys. But, that is what memories are made of and boy we caught some carp, fishing like that. The major downside is that everything that swims will eat maggots and so we caught them all, eels, tench, roach, rudd, perch and even pike. When the carp come in to feed they would knock everything out of the way to get at the maggots. It's really a case of persevering. We used that experience to great effect to catch carp from other waters but in the end, of course, it became too expensive to put out maggots by the gallon. I think learning to fish for carp this way at Keston set us up for life. I really cannot remember who but someone once said that once you had learned to catch carp from Keston it would

A young Ken Rowley with a Keston fish

give you the knowledge to go on and catch carp from most other places. I think that still applies today. I know a few lads that served their time on Keston and most of them have become very good anglers and gone on to catch some real big carp from waters like Johnson's, Larkfield, and Alders, to name just a few. The one thing that always makes me smile is watching someone you know that started out fishing for all types of fish and progressed to carp fishing. They usually become very good anglers because they are far more open minded and far more likely to change things if they are not catching. There is absolutely no substitute for experience. You cannot buy it or rent it. You have to earn it.

In those days, after work we would grab our tackle, fish the night, pack up, go to work then back to the ponds. That requires an awful lot of effort and definitely catches up with you after a few nights as it did on one night in particular. I think it

Steve Edwards . . . my float bobbed half way then popped up his then went under . . . !

was my third night in a row when Ken was fishing down to my left in the Funnel Swim and Steve was over on the Beach and I was in the Four Posts Swim. I had baited with half a gallon of maggots and the signs were looking very good. As the light faded, I could see patches of bubbles rising up from between my floats, the swirls of mist as the lake cooled created an eerie atmosphere in the beam of light that lit up the four posts I was fishing next to. I started to visualise what it must have been like for the people of a bygone age diving in to the cold inky depths and swimming around the pool. I must have nodded off because the next thing I remember was Ken shouting at me to wake up as he had heard my clutch screaming. In one movement, I lifted the rod and pulled into the fish but it tore off across the pool. The hook pulled and I was gutted. To my shame, I have to confess that during that night I fell asleep three times and not only did I lose each fish to a

Ken Rowley with the pet . . . AGAIN!

hook pull, but I missed out on a very rare and unprecedented opportunity to land three Caesar's Pool carp in a single night's fishing. I did however land one just at first light - a consolation fish of 16 or 17lb. That was in August 1968. Never again did I fish three nights in a row on the place. I feared my stupid actions had cost me possibly one or two of the largest fish in there at that time because I knew the bigger fish in would tear across the lake, nothing you could do would stop them and that was pretty much what happened.

There used to be an old boathouse at Keston in those days that was fenced off so no one could get inside. The reason for this was because folklore has it there was an

View across Keston from the beach

old tunnel that led down from beside the boathouse and went under the road and ended up in the grounds of Tate & Lyle. It was deemed unsafe by the local council and was fenced off for that reason. We used to bet in those days with any bloke (the bet was for ten shillings - that is fifty pence in today's money) who could stay the night in the boathouse. They had to stay until dawn. The ponds have always had their tales of ghosts, hauntings and ghouls. Little wonder really, when the area is littered with ancient burial grounds. I can honestly say that no one I know about ever stayed in there for very long, maybe a couple of hours at best. It was hilarious. First of all you would hear a person's voice, then a rustle of the pampas plants that were beside the boat house, then a blood curdling scream and the rattle of the six foot high wire fence that was supposed to keep us out, as a terrified teenager scrambled up the fence in an attempt to get out of there as fast as his feet would let him. It was such a laugh. We would all fall on the floor in hysterics as the boy with his heart pounding on his chest told of how he had heard whispering all around him before pooping his pants and legging it. Oh happy days!

In all honesty, there had been a few instances of ghostly happenings up there. I can remember one night when I was fishing the Beach swim. This is an area close to where the ice cream van used to park. There wasn't really any cover as you had the end of the railings to your left some fifteen yards away and a big silver birch about ten yards to your right. All that was behind you was a grass verge that came down to meet the gravel, which I guess was about twenty yards wide from grass edge to the lakeside. So, pretty much open during the night. On this particular night, at around two o'clock in the morning I heard footsteps across the gravel that woke me up. At Caesar's Pool you learnt to be a light sleeper. The worst thing was I knew no one else was fishing so I was getting concerned. The footsteps were getting closer and now I was petrified. It took all my courage but I put my head round the umbrella and there was not a soul there. Nothing! I even looked for a fox or badger but there was nothing there. The hair on the back of my neck stood up and I sort of shouted, "F*** this for a game of soldiers," and ran for my scooter. I had to try like a mad thing to kick start the bloody thing and I got the hell out of there in a cloud of two-stroke fumes. Jesus that was scary and I swear very real.

There were many stories concerning Keston Ponds - tales of a horse and cart going in off the road bank and the horse and the person riding it sadly drowned. That is the reason they put the railings up along the road. There was also a tale about a ghostly labrador. Apparently Sid the ranger had said the labrador ghost bit came about when some bloke had thrown a stick in for his dog to fetch amongst the lilies but it got tangled up in lilies and weed and had sadly drowned. I know Fred Wilton had an experience up there that he couldn't explain. Rather than me tell it, it would be better in Fred's own words then I can't cock it up and have to face the wrath of Wilton . . .

Emailed from Fred Wilton
Hello mate,
What happened was we were talking to old Sid the Ranger who said he would never stay at Keston after dark. Tony Judd said he had been by the boathouse one night, could hear breathing and thought it was an old labrador, but when he turned round there was nothing there but he could still hear breathing, so he threw his rods over the fence and ran home.

I told them of the time I had fished the night after working all day. I fished from the beach, it was a dead calm night and I was fishing in the margins, and I could hear splashing on the far side, which was dark because of the shadow of the trees. I thought it was the labrador and hoped it didn't come round to me. I kept dozing off, but the splashing carried on and something kept on telling me something was wrong, but my brain was too tired to work properly. Suddenly I realised what it was, despite the splashing there were no ripples coming out of the shadows yet the pond was flat as a mill pool. I decided I would pack up but I forced myself to break my rods down and put them in the bags.When I got back in the car I realised it was facing the spot the splashing was coming from and if I put the headlights on I would be able to see what was there, I decided I didn't want to see, so I backed out without the lights. Sid asked where the splashing was coming from and I pointed to the pieces of wood sticking out of the water, and he said it used to be a diving board and when he was young someone had dived off it one night and broke his neck, I don't believe in ghosts but that was a strange night.

All the best . . . Fred

Talking of Tate & Lyle, Ken, Steve and I used to go guesting down there. Below Keston there was, at that time in the grounds of Tate & Lyle, a small pool which

held a large number of wildies. For those of you who don't know what wildies are, they are common carp but thin, streamlined and powerful. They were the original carp imported for food by the monks and seldom grew much above 12lb. They fight like crazy and pound for pound would put up a much harder fight than their larger brethren. They are very rare these days as the strain has mostly been crossed with later stockings. We used to creep down there before it got light with a rod, landing net, an old, stale loaf and a packet of hooks. I can feel the excitement now as we would spread out around the pool and break off bits of stale loaf and throw them in amongst the tall straggly weed stems that grew in the pool. As it started to get light you could see the stems knock and sway as the wildies could sense there was food on the surface. Even in those days we would experiment with bait. It was known that crust dipped in honey was a good bait for carp, but we went further. I think it was Steve who came up with the idea of cutting an orange in half and squeezing the juice onto squares of stale Hovis crust. That again gave us an edge. It was so quiet there and nerve-wracking. Just the rustle of the rushes and weed stems as the carp made their way towards the bits of crust on the surface. In the early morning mist you could just make out their lips as they broke the surface and slurped down another bit of crust. You would sit there willing the fish to take your bit of crust, go on, go on, just a bit closer. Shaking like a leaf as a big pair of lips engulfed your bit of crust, a twitch on the line and you struck into a very angry, wild carp. They were not called wild for nothing as you would have to do all you could, hanging on for dear life as the fish tore across the pool making for the far bank. All the time, they would be thrashing at the water in an attempt to get away. Many a time we would whisper towards the fish and beg it to be quiet. Shush, you will wake up the gamekeeper who normally came down on cue at around 7.30am. This would be our cue to leave. Fantastic days indeed.

Funnily enough, when we used to fish for the pike in the winter on Caesar's Pool we would sometimes walk down to Tate & Lyle. The little pool was only about two and a half feet deep and would freeze over in the winter and you could see the wildies swimming around under the ice. In those days most carp anglers would stop fishing for carp by the end of November and start to fish for pike. It was widely believed that carp stopped feeding then and stayed lying dormant until the spring. How naive we were!

I haven't fished Caesar's Pool for God knows how many years. Ken Rowley still goes there from time to time to catch them and he calls it a walk down memory lane. I am going to make the effort next season though and try to have a night up there with a few of us, just for the crack. It would be nice just to honour our dearest mate Steve Edwards who tragically passed away on the 10th July 2010 after battling cancer. He, after all, along with Ken, taught me to carp fish all those years ago. I think a night on Caesar's and taking a walk down 'memory lane', as Ken put it would indeed do me a power of good.

The last time I fished the Pool was about 1983 with Ken and Geoff Tarrant. I honestly can't remember where I first met Geoff, maybe it was during the seventies and possibly from when I fished Brooklands and Horton Kirby near Dartford. Geoff knew quite a few of the Kent faces like 'Curly' Hatchman, 'Black' Paul, Paul Gummer, to name but a few. Anyone who knows Geoff will tell you what a very likeable man he is. A true stroke puller, comedian and on top of all that the man knows his way around bait. We swapped many successful ideas, back in those days when most serious carp anglers made their own bait. Geoff also happens to be one of the biggest practical jokers I have ever met. I can remember fishing the Pool one night in autumn when it was an evil night, gale force winds and torrential rain lashing down on the surface of the pool. So bad that it was all we could do to just put our rods out and we would never have got our brollies up in that weather. As luck would have it, Geoff was the proud owner of a camper van. Ken, Geoff and I were all snuggled up and warm in the van after having eaten fish and chips and were just partaking of a few brandy coffees. Geoff peered out of the rain lashed window to look at our rods that were only about ten feet away on the corner of the railings. "So easy to keep an eye on." Geoff said, "I think I saw your your tip pull round mate." "Really, I replied, are you sure? "Yes mate, definitely," he muttered. I thought I had better check and fought my way out of the van where sure enough one of my indicators was tight in the butt ring. I struck the rod, it's hard to describe the next few moments but as I lifted my right-hand rod the left-hand rod flew off the rests and smacked me in the side of the kisser. I didn't know what the hell was going on but I ended up with line round my head. As I looked at the tangled mess on the floor, I glanced back at the camper van and Ken and Geoff were wetting themselves at me stood bemused in the pouring rain. It did not take me long to work out that Geoff had swapped my spools over when I had gone for the fish and chips earlier. I flew at the door of the camper van but as you would expect it was locked and they refused to let me in until I had calmed down. Eventually like a drowned rat they let me in to get dry and warm. Such is the humour of some of the Kent boys.

Another instance of strange events that took place was when Steve and I were fishing side by side below the big silver birch next to the Beach. We had put a massive patch of maggots about fifteen feet out and we had one float each sitting about three to four feet apart - that's how we fished in those days. We were sitting on the roots of the silver birch watching as patches of bubbles started to rise around and between the floats. I can remember it like it was yesterday. We were tucking into some sandwiches my dear old mum had made for me. Big thick doorstep slices of crusty white bread with a filling of Bovril. Steve used to call them my mum's Marmite slabs. We tucked into the slabs as more bubbles hit the surface when my float bobbed and swirled. I hovered over the rod as my float slowly pulled down but then it popped up again and settled. Steve said his usual words, "You've blown it, Happy, it's gonna have mine now." No sooner had he said those words than his float bobbed and tore off. He struck, the water erupted and the fish went straight out like an express train. After a long hard fight I slipped the net under an immaculately scaled, big mirror of 25lb plus. Of course I congratulated him with the usual words in that situation, "You jam stricken, bastard Edwards, that should have been my fish!" I was of course happy for him, it was his biggest fish from the pool at that time.

Another incident that made us laugh was when we were fishing for pike one December morning. Steve, Ken and I were joined by a bloke called Phil White. In those days we used to use big bunches of lobworms for pike and Phil had a take, the pike tore off across the lake as Phil tried to hang on for dear life. His rod was bent double and the line singing in the breeze. He then started walking out into the lake and up to his knees in freezing cold water. We shouted in unison, "Give it line, give it line." To which he responded, "I ain't got no more f****ing line . . ." Well, we fell on the cold, wet winter floor, peeing ourselves as an almighty CRACK filled the air. His line exploded under the pressure. You see in those days we could only afford to buy spools of line in fifty yard lengths. Of course, once you had tied on new hooks a few times or shredded your line on a cracked, agate lined, tip ring you could get down so that very little was left on your spool. Honestly and truthfully we even tied our line together with knots at times if it broke. There were many occasions when playing fish you got a wind knot that looked like it would snag in the rings. Someone next to you would hold the line, bite through it, remove the knot and then tie it back together - you would continue to play the fish. It's called being able to adapt to any given situation.

It was whilst fishing Caesar's Pool that I had a chance meeting with John Carver. One of my friends, Dave Adams, who I had grown up with on the estate had met John as his then girlfriend worked at the same place as Dave. He mentioned that he also fished for carp. As John had just moved to the area, he was keen to meet people and knowing the history of Caesar's Pool I presumed he wanted to have a look and get some first hand knowledge on the place. Dave had suggested that we all meet up to fish at the pool. Dave, for a good reason, never mentioned that John ran Redmire Pool. Anyway we met up, and John had set up to fish close to the Four Posts. I had only gone over to have a chat but whilst there glanced over John's tackle and not only did he have cane rods, claw bale arm Mitchell reels, but also polished Bakelite Heron bite alarms. I was pretty impressed, but it was the landing net that got me. I really didn't want to make a fool of myself but Dave asked me what I thought of his landing net. I knew straight away that this really was a bit special. It was immaculate with a milled and polished spreader block. I can't remember what the arms were made of now, possibly ash, like the British Carp Study Group landing net I used to own but it was the handle that took my breath away. It was made of varnished bamboo and on the handle near the spreader block was a series of inscriptions all in ink and varnished over, of fish sizes dating back to 1960 or so. As you worked your way down the handle the sizes got bigger as it got towards the seventies. If my memory serves me well, the biggest fish weight was about 35lb or so and at the end of the handle was the name Jack Hilton. For those of you who haven't heard of him he was the carp fishing God of his day. Well, I may not have known who John Carver was but I sure as hell knew who Jack Hilton was. I tried to play it cool and act all smooth. I said my goodbyes and left them fishing. The first thing I did when I got home was to call Ken and Geoff to tell them that I thought I had just met the geezer who ran the Redmire Pool syndicate. My mate Dave confirmed he did run the Redmire syndicate, and told us that John wanted to meet Ken, Geoff and myself at Chipstead where we used to fish for the pike in the Winter. Straight away, I said that I didn't know why, but had a weird feeling that John was looking for decent members for Redmire and to this day, I have no idea why I thought that. Anyway, we met John down at Chipstead and we were getting on like a house on fire. We were all fishing within a few yards of each other so I thought I would try and impress him with my pike fishing skill and decided on a re-cast. Let's face it, he obviously wanted to see if we fished sensibly or why else did he want us to have a session together? I re-baited with a fresh mackerel, swung the dead bait back over my head and with the best of composure I compressed the rod and went to cast but the next thing I knew I was standing there with my landing net over my head and a stinking mackerel wrapped round my ear. Oh yes! I was out to impress alright. The three of them were on the floor screaming with laughter. I felt such a plank but had to see the funny side though. It was not long after that session that John invited Ken, Geoff and myself round to his house in Shortlands, near Bromley. I just had a feeling he was going to ask us if we would like to join and so it transpired that night when we agreed and became members of Redmire. That had to be a first - all three mates together on the same rota. I can't put into words how that felt. There was very little known about what went on up at Redmire at that time, just rumour and assumption. I will expand on this later in the book in the Redmire chapter. The people who ran the Pool saw fit to have a complete publicity ban on the place and as it happens, knowing what I know now, it was a wise move. The fee for fishing Redmire at that time was £360. That was an awful lot of money in 1983. I had never paid that sort of money before to fish any water and I have never paid that sort of money since. Back then there was still an air of mystery about the place and as kids we could only dream about the possibility of ever fishing there - those dreams were about to become reality.

Yes indeed, for whatever reason, Caesar's Pool had started me on the road to carp fishing. I had met people who would become lifelong friends. I had met Fred Wilton, which led me to use his revolutionary baits for a number of years and of course set me up to having a lifelong interest in formulating baits of my own.

One very scary and real incident happened up at Keston that could have put paid to me! One sunny late afternoon John and Roger Kemp, Colin Cameron, Trevor Church and I were cutting channels in the dense lilies, as that was the only way to present a bait. We would cut the channels about three feet wide from the margins right out to the edge of the pads. We would have to tread water to pull out the last few as the depth at that point was about six feet. On this occasion some bright spark suggested we swim right across the rest of the pool to the far bank by the four posts. As everyone started to swim across I swam at a slight angle and all of a sudden swam through the stream bed and the shock of the freezing cold water made me catch my breath. By this time I was having trouble moving as my Levi jeans, Sloppy Joe jumper, and desert boots were completely waterlogged. (Yes, perfect gear for swimming). I was going down, and felt myself go under, thinking it felt weird. All I could see was millions of bits in the dark murky water. I pushed for all I was worth and fought my way back to the surface. Now I knew I was in trouble. Panicking as I was gasping for breath and as I was going under again and I knew I wouldn't be coming back up. I felt a strange kind of tranquillity as I slowly sank . . . All of a sudden a hand grabbed my jumper and heaved me up to the surface. I gasped as I hit the air, panicking I nearly pulled my rescuer back down with me but he calmed me down and together we swam back to the four posts. It had been Trevor Church who saved my skin that day, and I will be eternally grateful for his heroics. Cheers Trevor where ever you are my old friend. Never mess with water, it will kill you!!

Yes, you could say that Caesar's Pool had indeed played a massive part in my life within carp fishing. What a perfect way to start this book.

Chapter Two

The Late Sixties & Early Seventies

The seventies for me was a time of mixed emotions. In 1970 I had just joined my first rock band, called Orion, and had also joined the Ashlea Pool syndicate with Ken Rowley. Ken and I had also been accepted as members of the British Carp Study Group. Steve Edwards, Ken Rowley and myself just discovered the Johnson's complex as well. If my memory is correct, the only other person to be fishing Johnson's at that time was Jim Gibbinson. So, there was a lot going on at the time.

Johnson's was an hour's drive or more in those days from where we lived in Bromley in Steve's trusty old Ford Consul. On our first trip I believe another old mate of ours called Kerry Patten also came along. I can vividly remember looking at all the water in front of us and thinking, Jesus this place is gigantic, as up until then we had only been fishing intimate, lily pad laden pools of around two acres or so. Now we were suddenly faced with a lake of around 26 acres - it was all a bit daunting. On our first walk along one bank we saw some great big boulders that were embedded into the lake bed but all of a sudden three of the boulders got up and swam off. They came back after a while and circled around in front of us and for the next couple hours we spent our time throwing bits of bread flake at them, which they completely ignored. They were so close you could see all the scale patterns. We were squeezing bits of flake together and dropping them right onto the flanks of these big carp. Not only did they not spook they just ignored the bits of flake completely. I would hazard a guess and say that these fish were between upper twenties and low thirties. In other words very big fish for that time. In those days you could get the use of one of Dennis Johnson's brand new fiberglass boats and a day ticket for seven shillings and six pence (for all you youngsters that is 75 pence in today's money.) I will expand on The Johnson's complex later in the book.

During 1970 I fished Ashlea pool just two or three times, twice of them in Jack Hilton's hide, which was a swim built into the bank by of course Jack. It was a bit weird fishing his swim as the man was and is a legend. You didn't need a brolly as the hide went back into the bank about six feet. My memories of Ashlea Pool are also quite vivid as one morning Ken and I were standing in my swim when the lilies in front of us parted at about twenty five feet out. All of the stems were swaying around and parting (to give you an idea of how hard it was to fish Ashlea there were only seven or eight carp in there plus the water was crystal clear and you had about three layers of lily pads and below that was a dense layer of cabbages. Presenting a bait freelined was an absolute nightmare).

Anyway the fish ended up about five feet out from the bank in front of me and masses upon masses of bubbles hit the surface as this big old fish ploughed its way through the cabbages sending up silt and debris in its wake. I was going out of my mind trying to lower a bit of flake down to the fish as the pads and stems shook violently from the carp's actions below. It was useless as I would only get past two layers of pads and then no further and as you could imagine my flake had just ended up on top of yet another pad below the two layers of pads above it. Eventually all the bubbling stopped and the fish just swam off out into the pool from whence it came. I can remember Ken and I climbing under a hawthorn bush once, and inching up to the edge of the bank and looking down on the biggest carp we had ever seen at that time, it was well over forty pounds. This size just didn't exist in waters back then except in Ashlea Pool and Redmire Pool. Ken went on to land two fish for that season, a 28lb mirror and a 32lb mirror that I think that was the biggest reported fish for the year and was on the front cover of the *Angling Times* or the *Angler's Mail*.

We fished all sorts of waters in the early 70s: Ceasar's Pool, Horton Kirby, Brooklands, Darenth, Johnson's, and parts of the River Medway. An upper twenty mirror had been caught under the old wooden bridge at Yalding so we fished there for a while. We also fished the Beggar's Hole - well that's what we knew it as but nowadays its called the the Tonbridge Ballast Pit. It was different then as you just fished anywhere that took your fancy and most places were day ticket waters. I can remember one outstanding catch back in about 1968/9 when myself, Colin Cameron and a guy called Bernie Taylor were fishing the top lake at Horton Kirby. We had wound in and walked down to the shops to get a couple of loaves of bread and on our return we were greeted by quite a large crowd that had gathered in front of our swims. As we looked out we could see what the attraction was because a huge shoal of carp were sitting on the surface no more than twenty yards out in front of where we were fishing. In those days we used to fish breadcrust that was anchored out in the lake by threading our line through a curtain ring, and then threading on a big bead with a size 2 hook to which the crust was impaled. From the curtain ring we would tie a length of 4lb breaking strain line about three to four feet long and then a 1oz or 1.5oz lead tied to the end. We would cast out into the lake, sink the line and then open up the bail arm on the reel and watch the line snake across the surface as the floating crust made its way up to the surface. You could either leave it on the surface or pull it down a foot at a time until you reached the level the carp were at (ring any bells?). Obviously it was an early resistance rig as the line would run through the curtain ring from your rod tip and straight up to your crust. The carp would suck down the crust and bang - possibly the first self hooking rig. (How many of you out there still think you invented the zig rig?) That was over forty years ago. Some of you inventors were not even born then. That day we landed about thirty carp between us off the top - an unbelievable result for that time.

We even had the odd bit of guesting when we fished a lake behind an old fever hospital, let's call it the Pea Lake. It was in the grounds of a huge house and we would scale the six foot high walls that in those days had broken glass bottles inserted into the cement on the tops of the walls. We laid our old potato sacks on the top and climbed over and into the grounds and then make our way past all these huge bronze, marble and stone statues. What an eerie place! On our way towards the lake we would occasionally turn round and look back to see if anyone was following us and our hearts would skip a beat as a statue would stare back at us in a menacing fashion as if to say how dare we enter the grounds of the secret lake. The lake was heated and come September it would steam as the air temperature dropped. You could hear the carp crashing all over the lake. Around 1969/70 we were using baits such as sausage meat with groundbait to stiffen it and usually wrapped around a pad of bread crust which your hook was pulled

Autumn on the Rookery, 1972

Late autumn 1974, the Rookery and Steve Edwards with the net

That's a nice fish happy!

That'll do nicely!

Part of a seven fish catch in an afternoon on lemon flavoured protein bait, 1972

through. Unbeknown to us at the time we were using the first critically balanced bait. I have brilliant memories of those days especially the smell of sausage meat that would fill the air as you made up another hook bait. We never had buzzers back then and the only indication you had was either a piece of silver foil wrapped around the line or an old penny piece on top of your spool with a biscuit tin lid under your reel. You either got an eerie rustling noise as the silver paper danced in the moonlight when the line whistled off your spool with your bale arm open as the carp tore off across the lake. Or, if you were likely to doze off, the penny method would be used as the clang of it as it hit the biscuit tin lid would make you jump out of your skin. Ah yes, those were the days. Our time on the secret lake was limited to between midnight and about 5 or 6 in the morning. Vivid memories of packing up, getting back over the wall and loading up the fishing gear onto our Lambretta scooters. They would be pushed up the lane away from the fever hospital before bump starting and flying off down the road on our way home. Eventually, as usually happens, we got careless and greedy for more carp catches. On one occasion we got so carried away watching the carp activity and catching them that we hadn't noticed the gardeners turn up at 7.00am. They immediately

Steve Edwards . . . the master at work

Ken Rowley extracted this one from the dense Keston lilies

called the police who turned up to arrest us. I think it was Steve and Kerry who got caught first but I was out on the island playing a fish. Steve called out to me, "Come on Happy, we've been captured." To which I replied, "F*** off, I'm playing a fish," as I thought they were winding me up. That was of course until I got my collar felt by a big old copper who, with his colleagues, took us down to the local police station where we were severely reprimanded and had our tackle confiscated. That was the last time we fished the secret lake but some years later after the pea people had sold the grounds we did contemplate going back there as we reckoned there would be some absolute monsters in there. Luckily enough, Steve had found out the property had been purchased by some villains and the only way we would have been coming out of there this time if we got caught, would have been on a stretcher. So we gave that idea a wide berth.

The seventies was a great time as I have always had a fun element in my fishing. Maybe that's my character or because of the people I have fished with - I don't know. We paid far more attention to fish spotting and climbing trees in order to gain vantage points to observe what the carp were doing. Time and time again you would sit on your chair taking in the atmosphere and tranquility of your surroundings when all of a sudden you would hear an almighty splash from just

Winter 1970, Johnson's Road and Island Lake

up the bank. The ripples would come washing back towards you. Bloody hell that was a big old kipper you thought only to be greeted by one of your mates waddling up the bank covered in silt, weed and soaking wet where they had fallen in the lake from high up a tree. I think we've all done it at some point or another, of course, we never laughed at their downfall (no pun intended), well not much.

It was around the season of 1971 that Fred Wilton allowed us to use his bait. I can only assume that was Steve's doing, as he had known Fred for some time and had become close friends. In fact Fred has only told me recently that he had let Steve use his PYM (Phillips Yeast Mixture) bait back in 1967. I can remember like it was yesterday when meeting up by the railings of Caesars' Pool and Steve produced a big cardboard box that when opened a cloud of brown powder escaped

The Magic Pool

into the air filling our nostrils with a rich savory aroma. It was of course the legendary PYM, used as a budgie tonic and full of vitamins and minerals (I think we ended up buying it in 7lb tins). On top of that when mixed with eggs and other base ingredients it produced a wholesome savory aroma. I dread to think just how many carp Fred's bait accounted for at that time - possibly hundreds. That first bait of Fred's was light years ahead of anything else being used at that time. I can remember walking round Baldwin's Lake on the Brooklands complex in the closed season and as I walked up the river bank I could see carp going potty. They were on the top and sucking at anything that floated, cigarette ends, leaves, bits of rubbish - anything on the surface. I just couldn't work out why they were behaving like it but everything became crystal clear once I had found out that Fred had been

Cuttle Mill . . . late 70s

round putting out his Equivite floater cake. A floating version of the the bottom bait he was working on at the time. Once carp had become accustomed to Fred's bottom or floating baits then no one got a look in. It was complete domination of waters in terms of what got caught and by whom. An unbelievable situation when you think it was over forty years ago now. I can remember Steve telling me that he had done the night with Fred on Sutton and they had caught ten fish between them. In those days you were lucky to catch ten fish in a season, let alone ten in a single night. So when they were asked by someone how many fish they had caught during the night they had to say just a couple, for if they had told the truth, they would have been branded liars. No one caught multiple carp in a night in those days. Such was the pulling power of Fred's baits. I can remember asking Fred if he thought carp would be able to find his baits in thick weed. His reply was, "Trust me once they are on the bait they will indeed seek it out and find it in dense weed or lilies," which indeed turned out to be true. It was the same when we fished the ballast pit in Tonbridge as we absolutely emptied the place. I can remember catching seven carp in about four hours one afternoon - unbelievable results for that time. We repeated that situation time and time again in the summer or winter. Fred was never one for standing still and no sooner had he perfected the PYM bait than was onto a much more complex milk protein mix. Using casein as the prime ingredient along with Equivite, a horse feed vitamin/mineral supplement. He also made his own blend of vitamins and minerals.

By about 1974/5 we were using food flavors as the main label for milk protein baits and around this time I moved onto to fishing a big pit near Sevenoaks. Two of my friends, Colin Cameron and John Kemp, had been fishing there for a few years so I moved onto there as well. The big lake was relatively easy and if you were on fish, you would catch them - at times in numbers. It was the medium size and the oldest lake that got me fired up. It was a much more mature pit and I already knew that Alan King was fishing there and had seen some very large King Carp it was a complete mystery lake. I personally had seen a huge leather carp that seemed to show more in one of the bays than anywhere else in the lake. Also one or two very big common carp were evident. The biggest issue was it was rock hard, about twenty-six acres or so, held only a few carp and had an abundance of natural food. I remember bumping into Lee Jackson on there and it was doing his head in. I remember Lee saying to me that he had fish over him time and time again but couldn't buy a bite! Eventually Lee moved on to another water and I even remember writing to Rod Hutchinson about the lake. It was a very difficult lake, but it got hold of you. Personally the harder a lake is to catch from, the more I want to fish it. I refuse to be beaten by a fish. Eventually we started to sort it out and my personal best season was about twelve fish, which I was more than happy with considering the difficult nature of the lake. In those days we fished from Friday night to Sunday afternoon, which is a hell of a lot of time. Unlike today, instead of sitting in a swim all weekend we would move around a lot. We only had cheap garden bed chairs, an umbrella, rods, landing net - everything else went into our Efgeeco tackle boxes. They were small, metal framed, tackle bags covered in canvas that incorporated a flap as a seat with a pouch on the back for our potato sacks. You could pack up and move in a few minutes. Your tackle box over your shoulder, rods, umbrella, landing net and bank sticks were put in the bed chair and off you went. That type of fishing can be far more productive than the very static approach. The small lake had some absolutely stunning fish in it. Beautiful heavily scaled fish that were as black as your hat. That too was a pain in the backside as, like the big lake, it is a wildlife sanctuary and you can only fish half of it. That's fine if the fish were in your half, but if they were not you may as well chuck your baits up a tree. Eventually it received more pressure and the carp would sit in the out-of-bounds areas in peace and quiet.

There was also a lot of politics going on at that time down there so it prompted me to move onto Sutton, which at that time was under the Hall's Angling Scheme. I believe it became better known as Leisure Sport Sutton. Steve Edwards was on there with Terry (Gaggy) Gauge and a couple of others. They had been doing really well just as Steve always did. At the time I was fishing with a couple of other mates, Norman Gatsell and John Bellini. Both of them had put a bait together that quite frankly went against everything I had been taught and believed in at that time, but you cannot argue the toss if you are catching and they were - big time. The first time I used the bait I had four fish in an hour. I laughed my head off as it was producing as many takes as Steve's milk protein bait, if not more. I loved the friendly rivalry and it was non stop mickey taking. Steve used to call us the Bellini boat people. Ha, Ha, Ha! I loved those days unlike now,which can be nasty, back stabbing bitchiness. We had a great season on Sutton and caught an awful lot of fish. One very interesting piece of information though, the bait we were using was absolutely instant and provided you didn't put too much out you just kept catching. The bait? It was ground up malt Shreddies with added flour and believe it or not 25ml of wild cherry flavor per 10oz mix - eggs were added and when boiled it dried out like concrete. Undeniably it caught fish left right and centre. Ha, Ha, Ha! Fred would have slaughtered me for using a bait like that. Funnily enough John, Norman and I decided to pull a stroke or two as at that time there was a baiting ban on there. We decided to hop over the fence at night during the next closed season and fill it in with the Shreddies. It took us hours and hours to grind down box after box of Shreddies, mix up the dry mix and roll it all by hand. Then we had to drive from Bromley twice a week with carrier bags full of bait and hop over the fence and walk round during the night baiting up. As the new season beckoned we were rubbing our hands in anticipation of going to stack them up like breeze blocks. The season started and surprise surprise we caught nothing, nada, zero, zilch. It still makes me laugh today about all that stroke pulling and effort for nothing. There you go, the old saying cheats never prosper comes to mind. Actually a valuable lesson was learned that day. If at some point you come across a method or bait that works, don't analyse it, just go with it. Use it and catch as many carp as you can in the life span of what you are doing. I think what happened was all the time we used that bait as hook bait with just a few freebies round it, the carp tolerated the very high levels of flavour. Once we baited it blew the bait big time.

By now, late seventies, I was spreading my time between the Johnson's Complex and I did a bit on Crayfish Pool and a few trips to Yateley. I hadn't really got a plan, I was just fishing here and there. I can remember walking over the field towards Crayfish Pool with Norman on a hot sunny day when all of a sudden we were caught out by an absolute deluge of rain. It dropped out of the sky like you would not believe and by the time we got to the pool we were absolutely drenched. And I mean drenched but as we got to the pool it stopped and the sun came back out. I should have taken that as an omen. I had to strip off completely as all of my clothes, shoes, everything was waterlogged. All I had to put on was an all in one thick padded suit - remember those? Anyway, as I was hanging my wet clothes up in the nearest tree I noticed out of the corner of my eye a group of fish not more than ten yards out in front of me. To be perfectly honest the only reason I wanted to fish Crayfish Pool was for that beautifully scaled mirror that Ritchie McDonald had caught at the time when it was over 40lbs. I had bumped into Ritchie in Penge Angling, he had given me a bit of information about the place and I also had information from Pete Springate and Kenny Hodder so I was quite prepared. There I was with fish in front of me and I quickly set up a rod with a candle controller and a cat biscuit for bait. I fired out a couple of pouchful of cat biscuits and straight away the group of fish were on them and gulping them down like there was no tomorrow. I cast way over the top with the candle controller and drew it back towards the group of fish and within two minutes the candle was away. The line snaked across the surface and I pulled into a very powerful fish which just tore off across the pool. It took all I had to stop it hitting a huge weed bed on the far bank but slowly I managed to get the fish back in front of me. I knew it was a lump as it was just a dead weight but all of a sudden the fish lunged downwards into the very deep margin. I felt the line give way momentarily then take hold again. I knew instantly what had happened, the hook had pulled but caught again possibly in the flank so all I could do was gently ease the fish upwards towards the waiting net. By now I could clearly see the size of the fish in the crystal clear water - it was very big. I prayed for the hook to hold but with the fish no more than six feet below the net the hook pulled and all that came back on the hook was a dirty great big scale. I had been right, the hook had indeed pulled and caught on the flank of the fish. I think we both knew what fish it was but said nothing. In the morning our suspicions were confirmed. The carp in the pool looked like they were getting together to spawn as a group of seven fish twisted and turned in their mating ritual as they made their way up to the surface in the crystal clear water no more than six feet off the bank. There it was, Ritchie's fish, and guess what, it had a big white mark on its flank just behind the gill plate where a scale had been. We looked at each other and packed our gear up and headed for home. I had indeed intended to return to fish for what should have been mine, but sadly some time after - I think it was Peter Springate or Kenny Hodder told me that they had heard a rumor that someone had caught the fish and moved it before Leisure Sport Angling took control of the water. Fate can deliver a cruel blow sometimes. At that time Peter and Kenny were over on Wraysbury so I dropped in and fished the night with Kenny. Nothing happenend and in the morning we looked across to the other side of the lake and a bloke was into a fish. Kenny said, "That's Dave Cumpstone over there." So we wound in and walked all the way round to see if he needed any help. By the time we got all the way round Dave was sitting in his chair eating his breakfast. Kenny said, "We saw you into a fish so came round to see what it was." "Oh, it's OK it was a pike about 7lb, that's it there he said!" As I looked down at Dave's saucepan there was a fillet of pike well and truly poached, half of which he had eaten for his breakfast. Well it takes all types, eh? Not long after that, it may have been that following winter, Colin Cameron and I did a few sessions on Yateley North Lake. What few carp were in there were quite active considering it was January and to cut a long story short we had found an area where a few fish had shown after dark, during the day. I had seen some swirls close to a small island at the mouth of a small bay which I was convinced were from carp. Someone had told me that 'Basil' did quite frequently get in that bay for whatever reason. We had gone down on the Monday to do two days and a night. Nothing much of interest happened during the day but an hour or two after dark we saw signs of fish activity and whilst I was sitting in my sleeping bag looking out into the darkness my tiny little indicator slowly pulled up to the top. I thought it may have been a liner but all of a sudden the tip pulled round and whatever was on the end shot off. I pulled into the fish expecting the line to cut through the water but it stayed firmly pinned in one place as the fish shot off out into the lake. There was all sorts of creaking and grinding on the line as the nodding dog on the end was shaking its head trying to get off. Slowly but surely I managed to get the fish back to about ten yards out and in the moonlight I could see the deep swirls hitting the surface. The corresponding bangs on the tip told me all was not well and then the tip bounced back and the line fell slack. I wound back to where my line entered the water and pulled and pulled until a dirty great branch festooned in dead weed hit the surface. At that time there were only two big fish in the North Lake, the Snake and Basil. Makes you wonder sometimes what you have to do to put a big fish on the bank.

Success doesn't always come easy. Some you win and some you lose. For years now I have had an uncanny knack of hooking either the biggest carp in the lake or close to it within a few days of starting to fish that particular place. Sometimes you land them, sometimes you don't, Carp fishing is very strange as you just have to dust yourself down and carry on regardless. Try not to get disheartened as I have often found that the scales of fate will eventually turn in your favour. My problem is that I just can't stay on a water for years and years trying to catch that one elusive fish. Life is way too short for that. I've seen friends of mine going out of their minds trying to catch one bloody fish. When someone else has landed the fish they are distraught. I've been told I'm fluky where certain fish are concerned, usually behind my back. It's usually by the people who haven't caught that particular fish, or because they are not welcome in those waters because of the way they conduct themselves. I guess that's modern day carp fishing for you, whatever. I've been catching fluky fish for forty-six years, and see no reason why that situation should change! In fact I am looking forward to the next one.

As the end of the seventies came it was a bit of a relief in some ways. The seventies were a very pioneering time for carp fishing, but most of the stuff you wanted you had to make yourself and that was not an easy option. Tackle is so advanced now, but not necessarily better, certainly not terminal tackle. That explanation I will leave for the chapter on rigs. The seventies was a time of immense change when the use of particles were on the increase. Up until the mid seventies high protein baits were on the increase as they had put so many fish on the bank, and every Tom,

Dick and Harry was jumping on the proverbial bandwagon. Bait companies were springing up all over the place to cater for anglers' needs, but people were starting to realise that you didn't have to pay a fortune in order to get carp preoccupied on bait. I can remember fishing Horton Kirby at that time and I was still using milk protein baits, but opposite me was a group of lads, who were absolutely emptying the lake. I think I caught two fish all day with my protein baits but these guys had caught about thirty carp between three of them - total domination. A complete role reversal of what had been happening over the previous eight to ten years. These guys were complete experts in what they were doing and how they went about it. Peanuts were absolutely emptying the lakes. (I will go into peanuts more in the bait chapter). The guys using particles, especially here in Kent, were developing ways to get particles out at distance by using old mastic tubes or Fairy Liquid bottles cut in half and gluing polystyrene in one end to make them float and upend to empty the particles. The other end had two lengths of 30lb breaking strain sea fishing line which were tied to a large sea swivel; some guys even glued fins onto the side to stabilize the tube in flight which also increased the range. Others even drilled loads of holes in the side of the tubes to make it easier to wind back through the water - what a great idea. These weird looking contraptions were called SPODS. Yes, another invention used over forty years ago before today's inventers of the SPOD were in fact born. Beach casting rods were used to cast out the particles at range. Some people even tied bits of elastic onto their spools so that each time they cast out their hook baits they would be fishing at the exact same range each time and where their feed was. Another great idea. Sorry, please excuse my sarcasm but, contrary to general belief, most ideas that some individuals think they have invented in the last twenty years were actually invented thirty-five years or more ago.

The particle era was a very revolutionary time but had its downfall, mainly because over the previous ten years or so carp had put on incredible amounts of weight due to being fed on high nutritional value baits. Some have said false amounts of weight gain. That is as maybe but carp had indeed benefitted from the protein era. They were in far better condition than they had ever been, sore and ulcer free, and heavier. But things were changing fast and not necessarily for the better, which again I will go into more detail in the bait chapter. As the end of the seventies approached a new era in both carp baits and rigs was about to happen. A very exciting time and some might say a controversial time was upon us. Carp fishing was about to witness some radical and groundbreaking changes. My own carp fishing had been radically changed during the seventies by anglers I admired, true pioneers like Peter Springate, Ritchie Mcdonald and Rod Hutchinson. Those blokes were among a handful of exceptionally single minded carp anglers who fished for the thrill, feeling of achievement and the challenge rather than the fame or financial reward. This unlike some of today's anglers who seem to prefer the celebrity status above the actual fishing.

Chapter Three

The Eighties

The early eighties was a fantastic time, things were about to happen that would change carp fishing for ever. Kevin Maddocks and Lenny Middleton had just invented the hair rig. I often wonder if anglers ever realise the significance of that concept? I can remember only too well when I found out about the hair, I was fishing Sutton-at-Hone at the time and most of us were side hooking baits back then. I do know that Kevin Maddocks had been field testing the hair on the Darenth Big Lake, and people were watching Kevin catching a lot of fish. Eventually one of the Darenth regulars found one of his rigs, which considering the time must have looked a bit odd to say the least. I think Kevin himself later wrote that he felt people were watching him fishing through binoculars. I don't know about that but for sure his rigs were found and the rumour I heard at a later date was that someone wound in one of Kevin's rigs which still had the bait tied to a piece of light line coming off the bend of the hook. Whatever! It doesn't matter it was out to a select few! Now one of that select few happened to be my old mate Steve Edwards. Steve NEVER, EVER gave anything away that easily, even though we were best mates. He would make me work for any information that would be forthcoming, and this occasion would be no different.

Like I said earlier I had been on Sutton-at-Hone since the late seventies. On this particular trip down I was in the gate swim when Steve ambled down the bank and said, " Hello Happy, mind if I drop in next to you mate?" As usual I had no objection, why would I? It had been a regular occurrence for as long as I could remember with us fishing side by side. But there was some thing odd with Steve on this occasion. It was almost as if he had an inner confidence of some sort. He just set up next to me, but instead of putting his rod rests in the bank as usual, he cast out with his back to me and just pushed his rod butt into the bank . . . "What are you up to Edwards?" I said. "Nothing Happy," he said with a smirk on his face! "I know you better than that!" I replied. "That rod will be away in a minute, my son," he teased." "Yeah of course it will," I said, "This is Sutton, what are you on?" No sooner had the words had left my mouth than his reel handle was spinning away like a Catherine Wheel! Back in the day we used to fish with the anti-reverse off and wait for the reel handle to spin as the carp headed out across the lake. Most of the time you were on it like a shot! But there was the odd occasion when the reel handle over spun and you ended up with a bird's nest for a spool and had to hand line the fish in. Not a good idea. On this occasion that didn't happen. Steve's rod tip had pulled down and the handle was a blur and he was into a good fish. I did what I always did and said to Steve, "Where's your net son?" He replied, "Don't worry

Stalking . . . the forgotten art! . . . Early eighties

They loved getting in there . . . so did I

They are out there somewhere in 97 acres!

Happy, I've got it covered!" I thought that was a bit odd but whatever. He dropped his net in the margin and continued to play the fish in to the net. He scooped up his prize but instead of doing the normal done thing of swinging the fish in the net up on to the bank, he unhooked it in the net! Then swung it up on the bank for me to assist with the weighing . . . Now I knew he was up to no good. "What you playing at Edwards?" I said! "Nothing Happy," he said. "You, my son are a liar," was my reply. We weighed, photographed and returned the fish; I can't remember the weight of the fish, it doesn't matter, that was irrelevant! He went back to his swim and just cast out again. The same as before and repeated the process, another reel churner in less than twenty minutes. Now I knew he was pulling strokes! Eventually we packed up and went home.

During the following week I received odd phone calls from Steve where he would say things like . . . "How far do you think a carp's throat teeth are back in their head Happy?" Or, "What do you think a carp does with a freebie before it deems it safe then bolts it back to the throat teeth?" Now I was getting wound up and he was starting to piss me off! I knew he was up to something but had no idea what! Then it struck me like a bolt of lightening . . . of course his bait wasn't on his hook but I thought it was tied on separately, maybe impaled on a separate small

The West Lake . . . the long wait for a take water

hook tied to his main hook! By now Steve knew I was on it so told me what he had been told by one of the Darenth boys. The hair rig had hit Kent.

We must have had at least a year or more using the hair before Kevin Maddocks published his findings. We caught so many carp everywhere we went. Unbelievable results. Steve stayed on Sutton-at-Hone but I moved off to the complex near Sevenoaks to plunder the spoils of the hair rig. That's where I met Mickey Dalton, bless him, he was on there whacking out a few. Most of us in the know were using size 8 or 10 Au Lion Dor hooks with two inches of 2lb breaking strain nylon hairs and were stacking up fish. Eventually the success of the hair became common knowledge, so Ken Rowley, Geoff Tarrant and I went back to Keston for a year.

Also we dabbled on Chipstead, where it became apparent that some big carp were present. We were on the tiger nuts by now and catching a lot of fish. Chipstead had a reputation for being a big pike water back then, and many well known pike anglers were on there but although we did fish for the pike, it was the carp we were interested in. We had seen some real big fish along the out-of-bounds bank (the north bank), but it was really deep there and sometimes over twenty feet just a couple of rod lengths out. That wasn't the problem as I had been catching fish in depths of up to twenty-seven feet over on Sevenoaks. The issue was that the carp could move so quickly and we could only sit on the mud flats and watch the carp start to show some three hundred yards across the lake just after dawn. Then they would make their way across the lake, porpoising all the way towards us. They would hit our area where we had three rods out each. You would get takes on all rods as they hoovered up the tigers. Three fish a piece if you landed them all and then they were gone! I never knew such nomadic carp! We would put out as much as five kilos of tigers each but you just couldn't hold them. A big shoal of carp would just come in, hoover up the food and move on. Much like Keston, they would follow the sun round the lake and disappear when it went down. Only Keston was much, much smaller! I think carp do that on a lot of lakes but it goes unnoticed.

Over the years it has become more and more apparent but the only thing that might change that cycle would possibly be angling pressure. Angling pressure on some lakes can change everything... The eighties was also a time of experimentation for me and I know for Steve Edwards as well. Bait concept was changing, certainly for us and I wouldn't be silly enough to suggest that the milk protein era was over. As it certainly wasn't as far as Fred Wilton was concerned. As far as Fred is concerned he still uses milk proteins for his barbel fishing and anyone who knows about the Wilton Wanderers' catches will tell you that barbel and chub are benefitting big time from his baits. But I digress. I know Steve, Geoff Tarrant and

I were looking into things like hydrolyzed meat proteins and alternative protein sources like blood meals, plasma, and soluble proteins. It goes on and on and on. The biggest problem is we were not fishing enough to work our way through all the product samples we were getting that were available. To formulate baits you need the biggest component of all . . . time and we didn't have it.

Sometimes I almost regret not putting in more time into sourcing products and trying them out, but there you go, you can't do it all as life has to go on. Also during that time I was in contact with Dr Keith Sykes from up around the Cotswolds somewhere. I believe he had some input into setting up Cotswold Baits. I really don't know much more than that, but one thing is for sure all the correspondence I had with him led me to believe that man was indeed a bit of a genius. Somewhere I still possess a huge bundle of letters from him with untold recipes, flavour/essential oil/amino acid compound blends that would blow your mind. We even had conversations about using hormones in carp baits that in effect would mean if you had a bait that contained certain ones of them it would trigger the feeling of pre-spawning. In effect the carp would be forced into a feeding frenzy that can be seen sometimes prior to spawning and then bingo you are in a different league. If that situation was viable and used in winter, then I could see some serious consequences occurring that I didnt want any part of. Steve even said to me, "Listen Happy, you shouldn't be messing with that kind of stuff as you don't know what could happen. You could rub some of the hormone gear on your head by mistake and in the morning wake up with a dick growing out of your forehead!" Some people said he was a lunatic! Personally I think that about sixty-five per cent of what he showed me and told me about was pure genius. He put me in touch with companies that produced all manner of products I had never heard of. He was responsible for revealing certain flavours that some seven or eight years later would take waters apart in terms of using flavours as labels which really did have the edge in terms of attraction. One company produced such classic flavours as victoria plum, chicken, and salmon. Ask Rob Maylin, John Baker, Dave Thorpe etc to name but a few about their success rate! I don't even know if Keith is/was a doctor and I don't care but that man was in a different league to anyone I have met, excluding Fred Wilton. He put me in touch with a company that produces animal feeds/stimulators/palatants. They produced natural sweeteners on maize bases, with aniseed infusion. Pig feed enhancers that you could get in powder or liquid form; I used them to blend with flavours to create things like the old Mental Juice. Anyone who fished the Darenth will remember how effective that was. When I think about it, that was about twenty-seven years ago that I obtained all that stuff from Keith.

Yes, there are some fantastic products out there now, but there is also a wealth of products that have been left behind untried or untested. If those products still remain in the same form with the same base ingredients, then there is a wealth of untapped additives out there for use in carp fishing bait formulation. There is one product that I know that Keith swore by when mixing with essential oils; it is an amino compound that blows Minamino clear out of the water! Most people have never heard of it, and most people walk straight past it when they visit a health food shop. All I will say is that it is used predominantly by pregnant women. When used with certain essential oils/molasses/amino compounds it can be, when used in conjunction with food baits, very, very effective. There are no end of things and products from the eighties that would still work big time today. You just have to be prepared to do the hard work and try them, and research is everything. You either sort it out for yourself, or be lazy and go into a shop and pay obscene amounts of your hard earned cash for ready made baits over which you have no control or real knowledge about. The choice is yours. The start of the eighties was indeed a great time to be carp fishing although within three years of the hair rig being

Colin Cameron one of the most successfull anglers on the West Lake

published, certainly on pressured waters, the carp began to start working it out. The Redmire fish had been hammered on the hair rig by Peter Springate and Kevin Maddocks prior to Ken, Geoff and I joining, so we had to find a way to have a go ourselves . . .

A Hilton pose with a West Lake fish

The West Lake fish never gave themselves up easily!

Black as your hat, West Lake mirror

East Lake common

Heavily scaled North Lake fish

The lake record for a while

Chapter Four

The Eighties Continued -
Redmire Pool

Redmire Pool conjures up many different images, meanings and realities for so many different people, and for so many different reasons. Each angler would have taken something completely different from their time there, be it just to sit and take in the atmosphere and the magnificent surroundings and tranquility, or to look at it from purely a fishing exercise with a chance to catch a few pristine stunning, scale, fin and mouth perfect carp of Leney descent. Without getting emotionally involved in the whole Redmire lunacy thing I grew up in an era when Redmire Pool was the Mecca of carp fishing. You had Ashlea Pool and Redmire Pool - I had already fished Ashlea in 1970/1 albeit for a brief amount of time, but this was different. As fresh faced kids, our dreams were made of Redmire Pool, the mystery, the history, the carp, oh those carp. When I started fishing very little was known about carp as there were very few carp anglers about, and information about them was extremely thin on the ground. If you wanted something, you had to make it, but consider this, two years before I was born Bob Richards had caught a 31lb 4oz carp from Redmire. Then four months before I was born Richard Walker caught a 44lb common from the place. Can you possibly imagine what that must have felt like? A bit like skating up Mount Everest on roller skates I would imagine.

That is fifty years ago, all but seven months, at the time of writing. A 44lb common carp all those years ago was, and is, in my book far more significant than the 46lb 12oz common I have just caught although I am not complaining . . . ha, ha. But, do you get what I mean? So, getting the chance to fish Redmire Pool thirty years or so ago was pretty special. I cannot possibly put into words the feelings I felt when we first drove over the cattle grid on entering Bernithan Court. Then down the track and through the field, glancing across the field to see the trees which shrouded the pool from view. Further down the track to the gate, to our left the dam wall, which we were destined to rebuild, and the old hut which contained the legendary Redmire Pool log. As we emerged from the van, an almost surreal headiness took hold of me. I am not a romantic man as such, but I kid you not, you could have cut a slice of atmosphere from where I was standing. The only unfortunate thing was that Ken couldn't join us on that first trip down, but his time was to come. Obviously Geoff and I were doing the tourist thing first - a visit to the Redmire hut, a look in the log where all the words and observations of the previous recipients of the syndicate were there for all to see. We were looking at carp fishing history - OK that's enough with that. Let's have a butcher's at the lake. Geoff and I wandered round the lake trying to take in all the scenery, atmosphere, passing each swim that we had only ever read about in books. We fought our way along the far

The wheel of fortune!

bank through the dense, overgrown, long grass and foliage. I say swims, they were not really swims but more like flat spots in the grass.

There were strict rules on some swims, pull back the willow fronds and tie them back while you are fishing, but undo them and let them return to their original position when you leave the area. Would you get that now? No some prick would gladly mutilate the area with a frigging chainsaw so they could put up a three man bungalow! The chemical toilet was also on the far bank, shrouded amongst the undergrowth. I can vividly remember walking through the long grass on a dew soaked morn, desperate to vacate my lower colon, and getting absolutely drenched up to my upper thighs. A change of clobber was always a good idea at Redmire. Once we had got the initial shock of actually being on the banks of the Pool out of the way the Kent attitude kicked in and it was, "Right, let's set about putting them on the bank son." Poor old Ken couldn't get down on that first rota as one of his company partners had a crash on his motorbike so Ken had to cover for him until the Wednesday, so Geoff and I were all alone with the whole of Redmire at our disposal.

We had a chat about where we fancied - I fancied the Stumps, and he said he would go in the Evening Pitch, just up the bank from me We were the new boys

You could cut the atmosphere with a knife!

so why not? We already knew that Kevin Maddocks had turned the place over the previous season fishing over tiger nuts, but fishing cream flavoured baits over the top. I believe Peter Springate and Kenny Hodder were on the same bait and had received their share of catches too. We also knew that Kevin had been kicked out of the syndicate at the end of the season or thereabouts - the old Redmire curse was afoot then? Well in our mind, why bother to fish baits over the tigers that the carp had been eating all the previous season, just go straight in with the tigers. Ours were slightly different in that we cooked ours in Langdale's maple and coconut flavouring. I used to put demerara sugar in mine as it speeded up the sugar and fermentation process. Well we knew not much had been out the previous two rotas before us, were things about to change? We also knew that the Redmire fish were not too keen on line, so we used Black Spider right through which sank like a brick. Ok, we couldn't cast far with it as it weighed a ton when it was wet, but we didn't need to at Redmire.We could catch them in the edge . . . well what can I say, before Ken had even got down we were catching. I had five fish in the first two days: the small fully scaled, the big fully scaled, two mid twenty commons and a high double figure common. I think Geoff had caught a fish from the Evening Pitch, but I felt that the fish were more in the central part

Me and a couple of local dogs, Prince and Muffin!

of the pool - namely smack in front of me. Ha, ha, ha, of course I wasn't taking the mick out of Geoff much. As it happened John Carver, who used to work for the British School of Motoring, had a head office not too far from Ross-on-Wye and just happened to be passing by as word had got back home that we had done OK in our first couple of days. John came down and shook our hands and congratulated us on our catches then went straight for the bucket in my swim to check out the contents . . . as if we would pull any strokes! "That smells nice in there," he said as he closely inspected the contents. He must have thought we were up to no good, which of course we weren't. John then gave Geoff some words of wisdom that poor old Geoff would regret taking notice of for some time. John said to Geoff, "Why are you fishing the Evening Pitch? That is the worst swim on the lake, it never produced a thing last season." So Geoff decided to move everything over to the Willow Pitch. I gave him a hand with his gear and he settled in and by now Ken had turned up.

Prior to leaving for the Pool Ken had asked if we needed anything, food, water, anything? We had both said in unison, "Yeah . . . more tigers!" Well you have to get your priorities right don't you? Any way Ken got down and looked shattered and we told him he looked like he needed the pub. To which Ken agreed and said he could murder a pint or two. I said we could as well, as my arms were aching from holding all those carp. After much laughter, Ken said, "I will just drop my gear in the Evening Pitch for the night, I can't be bothered to go any further." To which Geoff laughed and said, "You don't want to go in there mate, they don't get caught from that swim, Johnny Carver told me so!" (you just know what's coming don't you?). Anyway Ken set up in the Evening Pitch and we headed off down the road to a lovely little country pub, where we found upon our arrival an absolutely stunning barmaid who spoke with a kind of West Country type accent. To top that she looked as though someone had stuffed a couple of babies' heads up her jumper! Trying my hardest not to stare I said to Ken and Geoff, "What do you want lads?" I turned to the gorgeous barmaid and said, "What have you got darling?" And she said in her Wye accent, "Yo can have anyfing you loik!" I muttered under my breath, "You really do not want to be asking me that

Now that's what you call snowed in!

sweetheart," and Ken and Geoff burst out laughing. To cut a long story short we ordered a few pints and a steak and kidney pie each which when it came out, looked like someone had stuffed half a cow in a pillow case! Jesus what incredible food. I did ask the barmaid if Desperate Dan lived anywhere nearby, but she just said whoooooooo. Anyway, after consuming the said pies we waddled off back to Bernithan Court and a date with destiny.

By now the weed in Geoff's swim (the Willow Pitch) had grown up to the surface and was growing by the day. I have never seen anything like it in all the time I have fished as one minute the weed would be everywhere then a day or two later it would just collapse. Very strange, as were a lot of things we witnessed in our time there. Anyway Ken cast out in the duff swim, and over the next couple of rotas I think he landed seven or eight fish over 25lbs. Ha, ha, ha, Geoff was gutted. I don't think Geoff has ever let Johnny Carver forget his words of wisdom.

On the next rota down I caught another three or four fish, again from the Stumps. Quite clearly they were in front of me, and poor old Geoff was blanking over in the Willow Pitch again. I persuaded him to come over and get in my swim, and catch a few before we went home. Well that's what you do for your mates you fish with, isn't it? Share the love man . . . well I didn't quite expect what happened next. No sooner had I moved my gear out of the swim than fish after fish started poking their heads out and rolling, crashing, and bubbling over my patch of tigers. The spawny git only went and caught the nude leather, the big fully scaled, and an upper twenty common in the next twenty-four hours. That's the way it goes sometimes.

We became known as the 'lucky rota'. We would get down and look in the Redmire log and the last comments would be: Never caught anything, never saw a lot, looks like the weather is changing just in time for the lucky rota again. We were obviously popular! If I am honest, apart from the fish and the surrounding area, and the facilities at our disposal, for me personally it was an honour to meet the other guys in the syndicate: Peter Springate, Kenny Hodder, Geoff Spooner, on one rota and Barry Mills, Jim Hindle and Dave Gore on the other with John Carver as the floating member. As head of the syndicate he could pop down any time, which is fair enough.

The next rota down was a funny affair. Geoff had once again gone in the Willow Pitch, I had gone in the Stumps again, and Ken was in the unproductive Evening Pitch. Prior to going down, for whatever reason, whilst at a party over in Mitcham near Pete's house we were talking about ghostly happenings at the 'Mire. Peter was doing his usual best to glug his way through pints of what I think was Bacardi and Coke. Yes you heard that right, pints of Bacardi and Coke. Pete is well known for it. He was swaying in the breeze and telling everyone, "I have caught 'em all at Redmire," before laughing his head off. Which of course triggered everyone else to laugh, and no one could doubt that . . . he had caught them all. Then the stories started . . . the figures on the far bank, weighing slings swaying to and fro in the calm of the night, with not so much as a breath of wind around. I honestly can't remember all the stories now, but some were enough to make you think. Anyway we went down on the next rota and all went in our usual swims but we had a feeling Geoff felt a bit uneasy over in the Willow Pitch on his lonesome. I think the tales had kind of got to him in some way. Anyway we obviously must have crashed out, and the next thing I remember was waking up and looking at my clock - it was about three o'clock in the morning and I heard a crashing noise and moaning, swearing and whimpering. The next thing I saw was Geoff in a real bad state - he was a whimpering wreck. He looked completely freaked out, and as white as a sheet and kept saying, "There's a frigging ghost over there. No bullshit, my white enamel mug was floating about all over the place at the back of my bivvy." Ken and I were trying our best to sound concerned. "I am not going back over there, no effing way, that pitch is effing haunted . . ." Ken and I agreed to go round and check it out; I took a big torch and a bankstick just in case! We crept round and hopped over the stile into the Willow Pitch. I cautiously popped my head into Geoff's bivvy and sure as eggs are eggs I could see his old white enamel mug hovering around at the back of the bivvy. But, obviously I am made of sterner stuff. I put the torch on and there was the ghost of Redmire.Geoff's groundsheet was hovering up and down as was his mug. I pulled back his groundsheet and there was the ghost . . . a lovely little mole who obviously couldn't work out why he couldn't get his head through the wavelock material, and where the mole was moving under the groundsheet in the dark, it gave the impression that his mug was levitating all over the place. Needless to say Ken and I nearly wet ourselves on the spot, and to this day we have never let Geoff forget that night and the tale has been retold time without number whenever we have got together after a belly full of beer. That's when all the nonsense usually comes out, isnt it? That's what carp fishing is all about.

During the closed season John had said to us that the dam wall was in serious danger of collapsing as it was leaking like a sieve. Tree roots had fractured the structure of the dam, so we had agreed to go up and do our best to re render the whole dam wall. Barry Mills had gone up there a few days previously to drain the pool and when we got there it was an amazing sight as the water had subsided from the margins and you could see all the craters that the carp had dug out as they foraged for bloodworm or whatever natural grubs etc lived on the marginal shelf. Some were as deep as two to three feet, amazing to see it like that. The dam wall was in a terrible state with huge cracks that ran right into the structure itself. Anyway Ken was knocking up the rendering with waterproofer in it and I had the job of wading thigh deep in silt right across the face of the dam whilst filling any holes with bricks and mortar and putting on the first coat of rendering. The next day we finished the job by putting the top coat on and all that was required was to let it dry sufficiently so Barry could let it fill up again. I even inscribed our names on the face of the wall for prosperity. It's nice to know that we played our part in the history of Redmire Pool. That was twenty-nine years ago now.

There were many strange things that I saw at Redmire, some unexplainable. I used to enjoy going up to the shallows to float fish when carp were up there as it was just so exciting, I am one hundred percent old school for that. I would go up to either the cattle drink between the willow trees or the climbing tree opposite and throw out some lemon flavoured baits at first light with the intention of coming back around ten or eleven in the morning to try and catch a couple of fish on the float. On one occasion I went up to the climbing tree platform and climbed high up into the tree to see if I could spot any fish from there. If you haven't been there, then let me explain - I don't know about now, but back then at times the water could be crystal clear, you could see absolutely everything until that was the carp moved in to the shallows and started to feed. Then huge red clouds would cover the entire length of the shallows as the carp fed deep into the red mud on the bottom. An incredible sight, but strangely enough on this occasion I had seen nothing over the pool. Not one single showing of a carp, and there was nothing to be seen anywhere up in the shallows. I guess the shallows at Redmire must represent approximately twenty-five percent of the size of the pool. Where the hell were the carp? They can't just vanish . . . I sat up the tree for at least an hour trying to get one single glimpse of a carp. When all of a sudden I caught sight of something out of the corner of my eye to the right. Bugger me if it wasn't a Redmire scamp of a common around maybe 8 or 9lb. It quite quickly made its way past me hugging the margin, just skirted the margin line right round up to the extreme shallows, round in front of the cattle drink and willows and then it just vanished before it got to Pitchford's. Then about ten minutes went by and it reappeared, again from the right of the platform but this time much slower, occasionaly dipping down into the silt sending up a trademark red cloud. It again swam right round the extreme shallows and back in front of the cattle drink and willows where again where it vanished from view. What happened next completely blew me away and I couldn't care less if you believe me or not, but I know what I saw that day, and the older I get the more cynical I get. I have absolutely no explaination for what happened next . . . that same carp came back into view but this time right behind it was a convoy of carp ! In a perfect V shape behind the little scamp of a carp they passed in front of me right below in crystal clear water and I could clearly see: the fully scaled, the nude leather, the big linear, and loads of the mid to upper twenty commons - just unbelievable. They all filtered past me then slowly spread across the pool and dipped down to feed here and there. Until within half an hour the whole end of the shallows was a cauldron of red swirling clouds of Redmire mud and bubbles and swirls from the carp's tails. You know what, I never even bothered to fish. I just sat and watched the spectacle, unbelieveable, I had never seen it before, nor have I seen it since. Now you can say whatever you like but the only logical explanation I can come up with is that the little scamp of a carp was the scout for the rest of the carp. Once it had gone round twice to see if maybe there were any lines out, then it went and got its mates to say the coast was clear! Yes I know it sounds like I have lost my marbles, but I know what I saw and I have trouble believeing it too! But that is what happened.

On reflection, Redmire had been fished since the fifties and some of the country's finest anglers have fished it. It is only a puddle, isn"t it with nowhere to hide. How old are those carp? Donkey's years old. Who is to say that they haven't wised up big time? I do know that I hooked the big mirror on one occasion and I think it was Ken up the tree watching me play it. There was so much weed at that point in the season that it was a nightmare trying to land fish, but the fish was on the surface and Geoff was holding the net. So it was Ken who was relaying what was happening, and he said that bloody fish is rolling on the line and looks like it's trying to knock the hook out. Funnily enough, every time the fish rolled it was like a heavy bag of sand was being dropped on the line (ring any bells?)! The next thing the hook pulled and I said to Ken, "Was that a big fish mate? As it felt like a lump." He said, "It was probably the biggest carp you are likely to hook this season my son."

It's funny, I have been asked many times if the real big carp that were reported to be in Redmire were actually in there when we fished it, and as much as much as I would like to say yes - no I don't think they were. For a couple of reasons and for one there were too many good anglers on there that caught so many fish in the years leading up to our time. If those fish were in there, I am convinced they would have been caught, if not spotted or lost close in. The romantic in me would love to believe it but I think those big old fish probably perished as did Chris Yates' fish. The following year I dropped out and Bob Morris got his opportunity to fish there before the impending change of control took hold when Clive Deidtrich got his hands on it. Whilst it was nice to be asked to go there again when the Carp Society eventually took control of it I wish, like Peter Springate, I hadn't gone back, but I did, and to be perfectly honest it broke my heart. What was a lake in its heyday steeped in carp fishing tradition, myths and monsters had turned into a terrible casualty of modern day carp fishing. Instead of trees everywhere with the banks overgrown, there was a pathway round the lake like the M25 for people to put up two or three man bivvies. There was line hanging from trees, cigarette ends everywhere, teabags strewn here and there, and the biggest crime of all was that someone had nicked the atmosphere! The atmosphere that you could once cut with a knife. For me personally I can now completely understand why Peter declined the offer to return. I wish I had done the same and preserved those cherished memories of a once great piece of carp fishing history. I know it is easy to say that now, and I am also aware that there are a hell of a lot of anglers who will still go up there just to fish the place for its history and tradition. I suppose that if you cannot compare the Redmire Pool of today with what it was like thirty years ago, then of course it really doesn't matter what I say. You will enjoy what you see while you are there, and I hope you also enjoy your time on what is after all part of carp fishing history that started before I was born. Redmire inspired a whole generation of carp anglers from my era.

I think a very sad moment was when John Carver explained to us that we were about to lose the fishing rights to the Pool, as he knew other people were in a kind of bidding war to secure the fishing there. To John's credit he did say that he wrestled with his conscience over whether to renew the lease or not at the over inflated price now being asked for the rights to fish there, but I think quite rightly he did the right thing. Bear in mind John had been involved with Redmire for over ten years, and that the huge fish just were not there any more.

It's funny, there have been many things written about Redmire Pool - some of it reasonably factual, some of it complete nonsense. I had my eyes opened by some of the reasons why some high profile anglers lost their tickets whilst at Redmire by their actions. Quite clearly I can see now why Tom Mintram and John Carver preferred to keep what went on up there well away from the angling press. I have publicly thanked John for giving us Kent boys the opportunity to fish there. I know Ken Rowley, Steve Edwards and myself whilst fishing Keston only dreamed of the possibility of fishing the Pool, but John made that dream reality, for which I am eternally grateful. I am sure Geoff Tarrant, Bob Morris and all the other guys in the syndicate are also! Ken, Steve and I were going to leave the new people in charge of the pool a present in the form of a picture of a full moon taken on the dam wall. We were going to leave it pinned on the hut wall, but decided they were big enough arseholes already. I have only one serious regret concerning Redmire and that is the pictures I have of me holding Redmire fish bar one are complete rubbish, but I do have the memories to cherish . . . they are priceless.

The dream for three young lads eventually came true . . . at Redmire together

One of the linears . . . perfect!

Returning a common from the freshley rendered dam wall!

Barry Mills and Kenny Hodder . . . the quiet man, caught his share too!

Sir Pete . . . He caught them all . . . another one for Sir Pete!

Chapter Five

The Mid to Late
Eighties

Where do you go after Redmire? Well anywhere you go is going to seem busy by comparison, except possibly one water, the Ocean. Lots of unknown territory there, and uncaught fish too. It is of course a bit of a head banger. I had fished part of it during the seventies whilst fishing for pike so I knew where certain shallower areas were, but there is a lot of water out there that you just don't know about. To be fair most people who tackle it end up leaving the place alone. I think personally most people approach it with the boat mentality - row out find a feature or area and continuously bait that area with the hope that the approach pays dividends. Most of the time it doesn't. I only know of one person who has done better than anyone else and remained relatively consistent and he has fished from the bank. He has also put in a lot of time, effort and observation.

When Steve Edwards and George Mills fished it, they used baits that were mainly milk protein baits, they did catch carp on rare occasions but in general they were constantly mauled by the eels. I found the same thing myself. Fishing there at the same time were Nick Buss, Ken Rowley, Geoff Tarrant and Dave Lawrence as well as myself. I think Jim Gibbinson had been doing a bit on there too. I can't speak for anyone else but my plan was to fish the main feature on the windsurfer bank at some sixty to seventy yards out, which held a range of depths from six feet to twelve feet and was surrounded by an average of eighteen to twenty feet of water. For weeks I baited with a fishmeal mix, as usual it was the same plan of attack, get the carp used to finding bait in an area on a regular basis then fish it and stack 'em up!

Quite clearly the carp hadn't read the script. The first time I fished the conditions were perfect with a warm gentle southerly wind pushing right into the area so I was more than confident of action once the place had quietened down and all the dog walkers, kids, etc had left and the place had returned to tranquility itself. I felt like the night had returned some kind of normality to the place. By about midnight I heard the first fish crash, followed shortly by another. I could see them out in the reflection of the street lamps and I watched in anticipation as fish after fish crashed all over my baited area. They continued to do so until first light, without as much as a tug, pull, or jerk of the indicators. I have to confess I had been tempted to recast during the night as the fish continued to crash but had thought better of it. I was alone on a huge water fishing on a feature, possibly amongst one of the biggest features in the lake that just happened to have carp on it. Those carp have the option of swimming off to God knows how many other areas in the lake, so casting three ounce leads at them whilst they were crashing was not an option open to me.

Back goes another Barden fish

By first light all fish activity had ceased other than a few tench across the feature. Now was the time to check the hookbaits, and on inspection there weren't any to check. My rock hard hookbaits had been snaffled, That was about the last time I ever used big fixed leads - what a complete waste of time! Quite clearly I had carp all over my area eating my bait throughout the night, but it soon became obvious that the eels were to be a bigger problem than anything. No matter what I did, or tried I just couldn't keep the eels at bay. Eventually by changing to running leads it became obvious just how much of a problem the eels had become. Run after run from them when either you gut hooked them or they just tore your baits off your rigs. Even switching to tiger nuts didn't help as they ate them too in abundance. I think everyone at that time caught eels on tigers or anything that resembled food! Whatever you put out at range went. I started to fish the margins a lot hoping that I could keep the eels at bay by fishing depths of no more than four feet - out of swan depth but shallow enough for the eels to become less of a problem. Fishing one night a week on a water where by six o'clock in the morning the dogs were running through the margins where their lovely owners would throw sticks for them to fetch. It was fast becoming a head banger I could do without. I know Rob was putting in quite a bit of time fishing the margins to great effect but he was working on areas, constantly prebaiting, watching, sussing them out. Time and effort reaps rewards but time was something I didn't have. I have seen many people start with enthusiasm on that water but eventually they all give up. There are too many negatives about the place if you fish there alone.

There have been instances of tackle theft and violence. This is supposed to be fishing not self preservation. I think the answer might be to have say twenty full time anglers on there piling in bait getting the fish used to eating it on a daily basis. Then you may have half a chance. But of course you have the other things to deal with like divers, windsurfers, marathon swimming events, dogs, muggers, thugs dare I go on . . . On one occasion I had three rods out around one hundred yards on a smooth hard bottomed area and noticed to my right a load of bubbles hitting the surface, what the f*** is that I thought. Before I realised exactly what it was my lines pulled up tight and one by one fell slack . . . There were a group of divers out there who knew I was fishing but just ploughed through the area and cut all my lines off with a knife . . . tossers ! That was the last time I ever fished the place. There have been many Kent faces that have started to fish it but eventually they all leave. Sadly it's the situation that can make the place almost unfishable. Should the leisure side of things ever cease I would definitely go back but not in its present situation, oh no. From there I joined Nick Buss and Geoff Tarrant to fish a club

Getting amongst them on Barden Park!

in Sittingbourne. It is a small complex of lakes with reputedly some big fish in. Although there were some good fish in the small long lake, we fished the big lake and it did carry a certain mystery about it.

We caught a lot of fish, even through the winter but in the winter it became a quagmire of soggy wet clay that covered everything. The lighter sides were from the social side of fishing with Nick and Geoff, that was always entertaining to say the least, but there were a couple of abandoned polecats on the water who were, come the winter, obviously on the look out for food. At this point I only had Nick's word for it that the polecats actually existed, but I was soon destined to meet them. On this particular occasion we had the customary social drinking session sitting in Nick or Geoff's bivvy and the usual banter which always followed. Eventually I said my farewells and returned to the comfort of my own camp. It was a very cold night as I recall, probably December I think, so I just warmed the camp up with a couple of minutes of the stove on. As usual I zipped up the bivvy to make sure I wasn't visited by the fearsome ferrets or whatever they were. I must have nodded off because the next thing I remember was a weird kind of scratching come crunching noise. I remember thinking, "What the hell is that?" I'd heard a similar sound a few years back when fishing Sevenoaks and it turned out to be a mink eating a freshly caught perch. It was the self same sound but it was getting louder, and it seemed to be right above my head. With that I switched my head torch on and all I could see was great big claws and teeth cutting their way through the net lining of the inner skin of my bivvy. "What the f*** is that," I shouted! I took hold of my egg flipping utensil and started to beat the roof of my camp from inside to all manner of screams and commotion. Eventually I got up the courage to get out of the bivvy and was greeted by Geoff and Nick who were wetting themselves at my predicament. Unbeknown to me Nick had smeared sausage meat in between the outer and inner skin of my bivvy while I had walked up to the toilet earlier in the evening and of course the polecats had homed in on it and climbed up in between the skins of my bivvy while I was asleep. They proceeded to eat the sausage meat and the inner skin of my camp, bastards! I did however get my revenge as Nick had fallen asleep one night and woke up with one of the polecats in the hood of his sweatshirt. That was worth waiting for you I can tell you, I've never seen a grown man look more terrified! Then on another occasion Dave Lawrence was in my swim when we saw one of the polecats near his umbrella. Dave went round, picked up a bank stick and approached his brolly, with caution. He peered in under his brolly and with bank stick in hand started poking around inside. The polecat shot out from underneath his bedchair and bit him on the leg . . . I've seen some funny things in my time but the sight of Dave hopping about on one leg, swearing and cursing the polecat as it shot off through the dense rushes was right up there with some of the funniest moments I've ever seen. Funnily enough it wasn't long after that we pulled off the complex - the polecats had successfully kicked us off! Ha, ha, ha - who said carp fishing was dull?

I spent the next couple of years here and there flitting from one water to another. I was singing quite a lot then so fishing took a back seat until a chance meeting

A brace is always welcome

saw me on the banks of Cotton Farm at the time Gerry Savage ran the syndicate on it. I knew that Alan Smith had fished it so I thought I would have a go on there. I was at that time starting to make arrangements to produce my range of baits in a ready made fashion, so Cotton Farm would perhaps be a good place to start. I had met a nice bloke called Malcolm in The Tackle Box and as he fished the Farm, he agreed to show me round. He told me about the fish, the swims, and a general pointer on how to fish it that was more than helpful. I agreed to sort him out some bait in return as I would be fishing there so why not hook up and go on the same bait? At that time I was also trying to set up my garage indoors to turn it into a workshop for producing bait, etc. Malcolm was now into the winter on the Farm and catching with regularity on the winter bait - the Factor Seven, but to be honest it was anything but just winter bait. It worked everywhere and all year round. The time was fast approaching when I had to bite the bullet and give up fishing for a while to get on with producing bait, as Darenth was calling.

Keston in the winter

Chapter Six

The Nineties

It was during the eighties that I decided to start up my own bait company, I had been formulating baits for a few groups of friends for quite a few years. Not only was bait an interest of mine, since having considerable success using Fred Wilton's baits, but the more I looked into sourcing different ingredients, flavours, enhancers, palatants etc, the more I seemed to get embroiled in it. Anyone who gets into the subject of bait seriously will tell you that you end up spending far more time trying to learn more about bait than you actually spend fishing. It's just par for the course as you tend to rely more on friends and those you trust to give you information and feedback in order to progress. It's one thing to make a bait up for two of you to go fishing and try and have success, but a totally different ball game when you have as many as a dozen blokes relying on you to produce the goods. Not only can you not let them down in terms of producing a successful bait, but that bait has to be readily available pretty much on demand. I am not so sure it becomes an ego thing, as some people would have you labelled, but more of a pride issue. I would take immense pride in the fact that I had produced a bait that would result in all the guys I knew catching shedloads of fish, obviously in varying degrees as it is all down to

Mental Squad members keeping a low profile

Larry with the Mental Rig and one or two rods. Never let it be said we pulled strokes!

He's in . . . the bait's working!

The end result - what a fish!

how much each person puts into their fishing. Also, how good an angler they are, how much time they put in etc. We are all different, some guys don't have to try too hard to get results, for some it all comes very easily, maybe they are just naturally good anglers. I have mates of mine that really just don't put a foot wrong in fishing terms, but just don't catch as much as another guy who we fish with. That's life, in whatever form of situation through life, some will always be more successful than others, financially or otherwise, and carp fishing is no different. But there are ways you can improve someone's chances, and that is to give them a bait that they catch on, that alone increases someone's confidence to an amazing level. Simply because it takes away any doubt they have about bait in the first place. If you know that you have a bait which carp will readily accept, then that element of doubt has gone. You can then concentrate on the other elements of carp fishing that only you as an angler can sort out for yourself: location, rigs, set ups, observation, all those things I am afraid that you have to earn. There is absolutely no substitute for experience, you have to gain it, earn it, and live it. I come across blokes all the time who sit in a swim - they have all the gear, but no idea. I don't mean that as an insult to anyone, but it's a fact, somehow these people have been given the idea that you must have all the latest equipment, you must look like a professional carp angler to succeed.

I do love a bit of beach fishing!

What a load of old bollocks! Most of the exceptional anglers that I have ever come across all have the same thing in common . . . it's the man behind the rod and not what the tackle looks like. My old life time mate Steve Edwards (God rest his cotton socks) looked pretty much like a sack of crap on the bank, dirty old rods, reels, buzzers, everything was a mess really. He would cut bits of cork from his rod butts to balance his hookbaits, and didn't give a toss what he looked like, but hand on heart, he was the most successful short session angler I ever came across without exception. Steve had a certain mentality, and that's where I got it from, along with Fred's influence. Give them a bait that the carp will recognise as a nutritional food source and you are over halfway there. Provided you have a reel that works, a rod that bends, with decent rings on it, decent line, and sharp hooks, and accept that they will not always be feeding, then you are on the road to catching a few. What you look like has no bearing on improving your results whatsoever, I've done loads of stupid things in my time as a wind-up - I've painted everything I owned in camouflage paint, reels, rods, banksticks and landing net, buzzers, everything. At one point I covered my rods, reels, spools, buzzers, landing net in isotopes. My actual indicators were four inch long isotopes. Ritchie MacDonald gave me a big bag full of isotopes of all shapes and sizes, no doubt the proceeds of one of his little

They were looking for the Factor 7

tickles. My swim would glow at night. I think I had over fifty isotopes between three rods, reels and buzzers. When I fished the Darenth complex Johnny Bevan gave me the nickname Dizzy Chernobyl. I even had about six isotopes on my spools so that when I had a take my spool would look like a Catherine Wheel as it whizzed round on a take at night. It was all just a wind-up for those around you, but in order to do all that nonsense you need to be getting takes and putting fish on the bank. In order to do that you need decent, reliable, sensible - well I say sensible - but I mean good anglers around you. I am not sure I have ever fished with completely sensible anglers but that is not to say they have been irresponsible anglers. I couldn't have anyone near me that has no regard for the carp they fish for, and I have come across a few of those in my time. It is to all those blokes who I have fished with since I started carp fishing that I owe a debt of gratitude, especially those who helped me field test every single bait that I ever produced. Without their help it would never have happened. But the greatest thing was not only did we have such a laugh, but we caught an awful lot of carp along the way, and many a time we all achieved our personal bests on the waters we fished.

By this time I had met the legendary . . . Mental Squad . . . Gary, Dave, Nobby, Dougie and Larry, plus the Streeter brothers, Joe, Mental Melvin and later on, the

Larry, that boy likes a rucksack

Gary Harrow . . . he's a bit fussy about his set up

two Jasons. I don't think I ever came across a more random bunch of complete lunatics. But all of them were very good anglers who were only interested in fishing seriously. They had respect for the fish they fished for, and tried to put as many of them on the bank as possible. Now to my mind there's only one way to field test a proper winter bait, and that's in the winter! Get them on it in December and you have yourself a pretty good bait. Well it was very early December and I had made all the bait up in time for the start of the campaign. I did explain to all concerned that two weeks of baiting and fishing was required in order to get them on it. Have faith in it and you will succeed. Well, as predicted, just over two weeks of baiting and fishing and bang, it kicked in. Over the weekend Gary and Dave's son Rodney had something like twelve fish between them, and nothing else was caught on the lake except those fish. It was all over an article in the *Angler's Mail*, the following week. Not a bad start, but things were to get better and better as time went on. It would be perfectly fair to say that the boys really had it off, so much so we ended up doing a Mental Squad slide show around some of the meetings of the time.

As you would expect for Kent meetings, much humour, friendly banter and mickey taking, plus gallons of beer were consumed during these times. Kent meetings were not a place to be if you were not from Kent, as some of our northern brethren will confirm, you can't teach a Kent granny how to suck eggs now can you? Many a foreign body from outside Kent got absolutely slaughtered by some of the Kent mafia . . . during the old slide show days, you can't come to Kent and preach about bait and expect a serious response, it wasn't going to happen. This is the home of the invention of the nutritional bait started by Fred Wilton . . . I seriously miss those days as a Kent camaraderie and pride existed back then. The fishing was paramount, almost everyone got on. There was more respect for your fellow angler, a code of etiquette. If you went into a swim, nine times out of ten you would walk in the swim next to you and out of courtesy you would ask where the bloke was casting to. That doesn't happen any more, does it? Well not where I fish it doesn't. There really are some egotistical people out there these days. I've come across some anglers who really rate themselves - they seem to be wrapped up in this bloody celebrity carp angler nonsense. Get over yourselves, superstars are rock stars, and movie stars who are instantly recognisable in places all over the world. Not blokes who go down the lake and catch a few fish! Albeit some very nice ones. Foreign imports, although not new, were on the increase, instant carp lakes were springing up all over the place. If you were so inclined, you could go to a lake and fish for 40lb carp like it was going to buy sweets. You paid your money and took your chances. I am not so sure where I actually stand on the import issue. I do know that, along with many others in Kent, I kicked up a right stink over the introduction of huge carp into the Darenth complex. This was mainly because of the death of God knows how many carp that were originals that died because of the spread of disease caused by the introduction of foreign imports. It was so unnecessary, and if you think about it for a moment, the previous guardians of the Darenth complex, Liesure Sport Angling, had absolutely no long term plans in the way of a restocking policy, just as they hadn't with LSA Sutton-at-Hone. Darenth, to my knowledge, had not been restocked in years, and the only fish that went into Sutton were a load of small carp, and that year the pike all went up in weight by a few pounds . . . useless. You would expect a bit more common sense from a supposed large organisation, wouldn't you? What you also have to consider is that when Paul Davies took over the Darenth complex, it was effectively a dead stick and he had to create a business in order to bring in revenue to repay the loan taken out on the venture. In order to do that you have to attract anglers to fish the complex, but you can't do that in a water that quite frankly didn't have large heads of big carp. Darenth was way down in the pecking order in terms of boasting 40lb plus carp.There were waters elsewhere that boasted numerous 40lb carp that were now accessible, and fishable. Whilst I certainly don't agree with the way he went about it I do understand that he had no option but to stock the lakes with a new introduction of carp, and big carp at that. He didn't have a choice really to restock with small new carp that would result in people waiting years to start to catch decent sized fish. He was running a business not a charity. I personally hate what he did, but for every purist angler that only wants to catch so-called home grown carp, there will be three times that number who couldn't give a toss where the fish came from as long as it was over 40lb. I can remember one particular 'famous' angler who was well known for standing on the side of the 'keep carp British brigade'. When the opportunity came up to go for a big fat cheque as a prize for Carp Angler of the Year he toddled off during the winter to a water on the Kent border that holds a load of carp whose heritage was as dodgy as it gets! Don't you just love those hypocritical types?

I also have a major problem with all this Union Jack waving nonsense. The fact remains that there is not a single carp in the country that is British! They are all imports. The original stocking of the Holy Grail of carp fishing, Redmire Pool, was from abroad. The wildies that the monks stocked into monastery pools were all foreign. Where do you think Italian mirrors came from, Hackney? The fact remains that every single carp that gets caught today, from whatever lake you care to mention, originated from somewhere other than the British Isles. The best part is that from those original fish that have become residents of this country there are people who care enough to breed carp who have indeed produced some absolutely fantastic looking carp. What we all should be concerned and which has always been the biggest issue is what has been the cost of the imports to so many lakes in the UK? Well in my mind it has to be the loss of so many carp that died when these new imports were introduced, as most of them were not health checked. There was then a rapid spread of carp virus, and carp deaths were inevitable, but it is a vicious circle. Think about it logically for one minute. Mr carp angler gets successful, he catches lots of carp and then decides to write about his success story. This in turn gets more people from either other branches of angling, or people who see his catches or read about his exploits and they then want some of it. Of course business people think, hang on a minute there's an angle here, (no pun intended) we could make a lot of money out of this carp fishing lark. Angling continues to be the biggest participatory sport in the country, so they will need tackle, bait, rods etc and of course they will need somewhere to fish for those carp. OK, lets buy a few lakes and fill them with 40lb carp. People will want to catch a 40 or even 50lb. carp and those who can afford it won't give a toss where they have come from. Am I so wrong? Of course not, carp fishing is big business these days so please don't get all patriotic over something which was never British in the first place. The very real fact of the matter is that every single person who has ever written for a carp fishing magazine has in some way contributed to the rise in popularity of carp fishing, which in turn has involved a demand to provide lakes for all the carp anglers who want to catch huge carp, irrespective of their origins. Yes, of course, there are the purists who in their own deluded way want to voice an opinion and wave their Union Jacks and shout, "Keep carp fishing British!" Sorry to disappoint you lads but there is no such thing technically as a British carp! That is one of the biggest issues of the nineties to my mind. How you see it is of course your choice, and of course there is nothing wrong with wanting to prevent even more imports coming into the country, but you may just find that it is too late. I would dearly love to know how the purists can now tell the difference between a so-called British carp (which doesn't actually exist) and a so-called import. There were some fantastic looking carp introduced into the Darenth complex, low twenties in weight, I am not sure if I am totally correct but I think they came from Hungary. Ironically not far away from where the Redmire Galician carp came from. They really are a fantastic looking strain of carp, beautiful, and quite nicely scaled fish with a kind of chestnut colouring to them. Obviously they darken down to their surroundings, but I would defy any one of the purists to tell the difference between a so-called import from Hungary and a so-called home grown British carp. Obviously I use the term British very loosely. I haven't bought a weekly carp fishing magazine for about ten years now, but when I do glance through one a friend has bought, quite clearly it is obvious that some of these carp in their upper thirties and low forties look incredibly like the same strain of Hungarian carp that went into the Darenth complex. The only difference being that the carp are being reported as coming from all over the country. Does anyone really know if a handful of low twenty scaley looking carp have been introduced into a water? I doubt it. I have to say that if I had a lake, and I had access legally to some Hungarian strain carp that in my opinion, looked like they had the potential to grow to a decent size and were very good looking fish, then I would definitely have them, and I wouldn't care less what the purists thought. If you don't like it, then fish somewhere else, you pay your money and choose. I can, however, see the need for tougher legislation on imports and if waving a Union Jack around helps that cause then well done you, but don't expect everyone to hold the same opinions as you.

Here is an interesting tale for you . . . when I lived in Keston, I obtained a batch of small carp from World of Koi in Oakley Road. I saw them in their tanks and I thought to myself that they looked like they had the potential with their body shape and nice scaling to become possibly big fish with the right start in life. They were approximately three inches long and I paid fifty pence each for them and bought twenty-five. They actually came from a large local pond in someone's garden that the World of Koi were asked to net and remove the carp as they were overrunning the pond. I took them home to my koi pond and fed them on my own fish protein bait in floater cake form that was based on LT94 herring meal. It was some twenty-four years ago now and I fed them three times a day. Within four years the largest wasn't far short of twenty pounds and they were stunning fish. Some pure linears, a couple of fully scaled fish and amongst them there was a group of about seven that had a kind of fungus on them - it wasn't carp pox, or any kind of virus but just a kind of hue across their backs, shoulders and slightly down their flanks. Well eventually I had to move and didn't have the facility to keep them, so I arranged to sell them to Ian Welch who ran Leisure Sport Angling at the time. I was paid £600 for the whole contents of my pond. I can't remember how many carp now, but certainly in excess of fifty. I know Del, the head bailiff at Horton, wanted some for there, and I know for a fact that a few went into Wraysbury including for certain the ones with the fungus on them. You know they became known as the 'fungus family', and the biggest fish is now known as King Fungus. I believe it has been caught at around 47 or 48lb now - what a turn up for the book (no pun intended). Guess what? I recently read up about King Fungus on the Cemex Angling website and apparently that fish is a pure Leney! Wow how about that! Incredible, King Fungus has gone from my garden koi pond to being a thoroughbred Leney carp. I did send an email to Cemex Angling suggesting that they had it all wrong and King Fungus was nothing of the sort. Strangely enough I never got an email from them in reply . . . funny that eh? I guess people or companies who own lakes have the inhabitants labelled as whatever they want them to be. That is why I am so sceptical concerning origins of carp. The fact of the matter is we never really know 100 percent where some of the carp we fish for really come from, do we?

During the early nineties I was having so much fun as I was producing baits that were fast becoming known for their ability to put fish on the bank. It was such a laugh. The old bait firm rivalry was rife and especially on the Darenth complex. You had Premier Baits who to their credit had turned the angling bait world on its head because the fish captures their products had accounted for were outstanding and the weights the carp were packing on due to the quantity and quality of their products was just incredible. Then you had Martin Locke's Solar Baits that were also catching more than their fair share. I was in the middle somewhere. Originally my bait firm was called Buttcracker Baits, but I had to change the name for fear of upsetting my lifelong mate Steve Edwards as he was known in very discreet

King Fungus . . . 11lb day of stocking into Wraysbury . . . the little acorn!

. . . and caught by Phil Bunyan at 47lb . . . the mighty oak!

ultracult circles as Buttcracker and was offended by the fact. Although it was after all a term for a take in those days, it wasn't worth falling out over so I changed the name out of respect for our friendship.

I have many fond memories of those days, as I said, bait company wars were rife. Some took it far more seriously than others, not I hasten to add the proprietors of the bait companies but more the anglers who used their products. I think the best times were when the winters had set in. With the old fishmeal baits, which at the time were in fashion, the norm was to glug the freebies in copious amounts of fish oil. Obviously during the very cold months that oil would turn into a kind of lardy looking substance in the bait bag that of course gave substance for all manner of mickey taking when my mates were fishing the Tip Lake on my old Factor Seven mix. The old fishmeal baits, although highly successful during warmer temperatures, were starting to slow right down in terms of captures, and once you get a decent birdfood/high fibre bait established in the winter it is very hard to compete with it. All the time there was the mickey taking. My old muckers, big Ted Bryant and Graham Hackett, were relentless in verbally abusing the Premier lads, especially Ollie or Johnny Bevan. Ted would say to Ollie, "Here mate you don't have any of that nod oil on you, do you?" And Ollie would say, "Why, do you want to use some proper stuff?" And Ted would say, "No mate, I just want to oil my reels." This was usually followed by the sound of copious amounts of laughter. Then as it got really cold, if Ted saw Ollie or John coming towards them, he would light a candle and pour the molten wax all over the floor in a big puddle as they staggered past his swim all loaded up with tackle. When they got a way up the bank he would call them back and say, "I think you have dropped something on the floor," and he would point to the wax on the floor and say, "Have you spilt your nod oil?" This again was to much howling of laughter from all around. Now Ollie used to love a kip, he could sleep for England, and Ted would wait till Ollie was sound asleep and snoring like a chainsaw, and then he would walk up to his bivvy and shout through the door, "Ollie . . . Ollie, wake up, he's caught one!" To which Ollie would awake from his deep sleep and say, "Who's caught one?" To which Ted would reply, "Ian Botham . . . see you later!" Ted would get him in the middle of the night at all hours and tormented him all the time. I have to say that they were some of the funniest days I have ever spent fishing, but that was all down to the characters on the bank.

Some of the old British Carp Study Group meetings which were held at Orchid Lakes or Dorchester Lagoon each year were outrageous events. Those were the days when it was worth being in the BCSG. Most of the country's best anglers were members back then - an Annual General Meeting would mean the likes of

Mike Willmott, Peter Springate, Kenny Hodder, a very young Dave Gawthorn, John Baker, Brian Jarrett. I just can't remember all the blokes here and now but it would be, put up the camp, set up, then arange for everyone to meet up the local pub, that would graciously open for us and lock us in until the very early hours. On being evicted we would have to stagger back through the inky darkness trying to find our way back to our swims and it never really worked out as planned. One year I can vaguely remember staggering back and Dave Gawthorn, who was celebrating being accepted into the BCSG, was so pissed he tried to manouvre his way round a tight bend of someone's hedge but missed completely and ended up going right through the hedge face first! What a state, all you could see was a little pair of legs hanging out of the hedge . . . we dragged him out and his face looked like Madam Sin had bashed his boat race with a metal rake. Those were the days . . . make no mistake. Oh dear, thanks for the memories, irreplacable memories, of camaraderie and carp fishing friendships that stand the test of time to be recounted on numerous occasions.

There was a drinking culture back then in carp fishing, but I would have to say that you were either drinking, or fishing, very seldom did you do both. Yes, I know there was the odd occasion that was bordering on the ridiculous, but I never ever remember being drunk and fishing with my rods out at the same time. He says with a straight face! That is irresponsible, unlike today when I've seen blokes either drinking at eight o'clock in the morning, or they have been completely out of it on gear. I think it applies more to the long term anglers. I suppose you need something to keep you going day in day out, sod that for a game of soldiers. I've got a life. I have seen a lot of blokes implode due to constant carp fishing; it's the old adage of suffering from burn out! Carp fishing has produced a long line of burn out victims. Some blokes today are in the relentless pursuit of monster carp and the so called fame that comes with it and it certainly takes its toll on some individuals. I've seen blokes who once looked fresh faced and who enjoyed their fishing turn into carp fishing casualties that look ten years older than they actually are. Each to their own, eh? The nineties, to me personally, were definitely amongst the most enjoyable times. More people fished in groups then and I think it was accepted that logically you were able to learn more about the lake you were fishing, its inhabitants, and the underwater world we knew little about. The shared knowledge that was gained by pooling your experiences, and of course you could have up to eight or ten blokes all on the same bait, which in those days was a huge advantage. I am not so sure it applies any more as there are too many variables in today's style of carp fishing.

Cotton Farm illuminations . . . surreal!

Plus, of course, unless you are in the know, a baiting campaign can be a seriously expensive liability these days, and there is no gaurantee any more of getting the lion's share of the action by piling in the bait. I have seen it loads of times in the last few years - a group of guys get together and absolutely fill the lake in with bait only to be completely out fished by a group of four guys piling in hemp that is processed one way or another to make it different. That I think is the key nowadays - doing something very different to what everyone else is doing. It is not always as difficult to do as it sounds. Back in those days you tended to get groups of anglers doing something different to the next group of anglers, that kind of made things more interesting. Plus not one individual thing got overused too soon. It meant that you got a spread of captures of carp on different methods, baits, rigs, etc. I don't think it is like that any more what with all the social media - magazine articles desperate to publish the latest so called edge, be it a rig, bait, method, whatever. I think once a fashionable edge gets out, then it spreads like wildfire which also means that everyone gets on it much quicker making the effectiveness of that so called edge very short lived. Whereas twenty years ago a particular edge could probably get you three seasons' worth of fishing

The sun sets over the industrial units at the Farm

with an advantage before it started to become well known. I remember the start of the season on the Darenth complex back in about 1989/90. Hardly anything was being caught and then all of a sudden Gary Prosser caught an absolute hatful of fish. Quite clearly he had sorted out a method giving him some considerable advantage. I don't know if it was Gary's idea or not but what he had going was certainly a serious edge. Things were very secretive back then, but once I had been shown what the fuss was all about, everything became crystal clear. Then you could see why and how others that thought they had twigged it were in fact so far off the mark that it was hilarious. Gary was using the very first so-called zig rig that every Tom, Dick and Harry claims to have invented in the last five years. To this day, in my humble opinion, there is no zig rig which does what Gary's was doing, or what it does today, in terms of versatility. As far as I know that method had not been used anywhere else although we had used anchored floater cake at all depths in order to catch fish since the sixties. That was the first so-called zig rig over forty years ago, but it was still not as versatile as the rig Gary was using. You fished as normal with a lead set up but with a long hooklink set at whatever depth you thought carp were cruising at. Say eight feet up in twelve feet of water, but on the end of your hooklink you had a pop-up tight to the bend of the hook, and a slideable counter balance four inches from your hook. Once you had critically balanced your hook bait you then slid the counterbalance back down to the lead end which you set at about three inches from the lead. Then you stuck your hookbait in a large mug, dropped a sheet of pva over the hookbait and then you put the coils of line carefully on top ready for you to cast with ease. Once out there the counterbalance acted as a confidence rig. As the carp dropped down over the balanced hookbait and sucked, so the hookbait lifted into the carp's mouth and it was snookered as the minute the carp went to upright itself it was straight onto the lead and fairly hooked in the bottom lip. Game over. The funniest thing was that no one seemed to look at the lead as you played the carp to the net and never noticed the tiny counter balance set three inches from the lead. So, lots and lots of people assumed that the edge was a six or eight foot hooklink. I was even told one day by one of the local lads " . . . pssst I know what Gary Prosser is doing! He is using six to eight feet hooklinks with a bottom bait." I had a job keeping a straight face, but never let on. I would have been hung, drawn and quartered by the Kent mafia. That set up in my opinion is much better than the commercially made zig rigs of today. Given the option of chucking out lumps of plastic all in pretty shapes and colours or putting out a bait they are eating off the bottom all day long that you control the effectiveness of - give me the bait every time over plastic or foam, which is just plain lazy and convenience fishing in my opinion.

I suppose that is the biggest edge us old timers have these days; you can actually draw from a wealth of information and set ups or methods that are considered old hat or out of date. Just because something hasn't been used for twenty years or so doesn't make it any less effective. Some of the best ideas I have ever seen were born in the 90s, mainly because the materials that were being made available to carp fishing were allowing those pioneers of that time to really utilise their ideas. I worked up in London at the time and I know that Steve Edwards and I tried to utilise eye sutures which were being used in eye surgery. They were very, very strong braided type material, but so smooth, and fine, possibly the thickness of 1lb nylon line, but with the strength of about 8lb breaking strain. The biggest problem was that the sample lenghts were no more than about three inches long. Enough for a few stitches but not for a hooklink. If we had been loaded, we would have tried to purchase the stuff in longer lengths but try asking a major company to sell you a 100yd spool of this gear for eye surgery and they laugh at you. Yes, the 90s were indeed a very interesting and revolutionary time!

It was during the winter that my first commercial ready made bait started to account for fantastic results. I had been field testing the bait, (Factor 7) on Cotton Farm, a water which is now well known for being the home of the big common, sadly no longer alive. At the time it was controlled by Gerry Savage and to be perfectly honest I didn't pay for a ticket, as such, as I was sending Gerry the equivalent in bait, ingredients and flavours so no cash actually changed hands. At the time the late, great Alan Smith had been putting in his milk protein mix with geranium oil and as you would expect of Alan he was catching loads. So it would have been pointless trying to go down that road as I wanted to prove to myself that going to the complete opposite end of the bait spectrum would prove an advantage. I had for some time felt that milk proteins were becoming less and less effective, not only as they were now so expensive in that to produce a decent bait would eventually prove financially unviable. I had already learned that the introduction of too much milk protien in one lake had proved to be a bit of a disaster, which I will elaborate on in the bait section. Not because of iffy ingredients but in terms of digestion. Anyway, I had decided to introduce a bird food blend of ingredients which included a rearing food from Holland which I knew had not been pursued by any bait companies. The only supplier I know of in this country and who I have dealt with for over twenty-five years has told me that he has never been approached by a bait company asking for that product. It really surprised me but also made me very happy as sometimes just having something different in terms of an ingredient could, and has been, a big advantage in terms of results on the bank. It doesn't have to cost a fortune to make it effective either. I had shared my bait with a very nice bloke called Malcolm, a very quiet unassuming bloke, but who clearly knew the water and had caught loads of fish from there previously. To cut a long story short Malcolm was really starting to catch them on the new bait. In fairness I had been put onto a particular blend of two flavours and an aminno-acid blend that had already emptied numerous waters up in the Colne Valley region by two old school carp fishing legends who shall remain nameless, and so will the blend. As it wasn't my idea, nor was it my combination of flavours/ammino acid blends, plus I like my front teeth just the way they are thank you very much! I knew from the start that the birdfood, flavour, ammino blend, sweetener combination would work from the off. Martin Locke was doing something similar with his own combination and, as you would expect of Martin, would also be stacking them up where he was fishing. So the word field testing didn't really apply in the true context of things. But I did need to have other blokes using the bait so it could be seen by the general public fishing alongside my friends that the bait did indeed work, and was putting more than its fair share of carp on the bank. So I guess Cotton Farm and the Darenth complex were the very first waters to be used as a testing ground for my baits by other anglers and that was always a bit daunting as you want them to do well. There is also the fear of failure and I had plenty of failures under my belt during the previous fifteen or more years due to duff ingredients. It's a killer, you can end up having three months of completely wasted time and effort just by having sub standard or out of date ingredients in your bait. Just one ounce of a duff ingredient in your bait is enough to render it useless. Again I will expand on that situation in the bait section. It transpired that I was worrying needelessly as the bait was starting to do the business wherever it was being used. As I said earlier, I wanted the bait to be used and field tested during the winter (December to March) because if you get results then, you are in a winning

Dougie Jones! Not quite right in the head!

One of many fish from Cotton

Returning a Cotton Farm original

situation. Proof beyond doubt that it works. I was now entering into a realm of the unknown, the world of backstabbing, competition for bragging rights, bait wars, lies, deceit, dirty tricks. Oh yes, welcome to the world of bait companies. You would be really surprised at the dirty tricks used by certain individuals in order to try and discredit certain bait companies, When I look back at some of the lies and rumours put around during those times it makes my hair curl (what's left of it) but that was then, this is now. I will move swiftly on to the Darenth complex and the mental squad - a time in my life of so much fun, laughter and meeting so many outstanding anglers, so many absolutely crazy geezers who I found not only inspiring, but with whom I hope I have forged friendships that have stood the test of time . . .

Lockie's reaction when refused MENTAL SQUAD membership lol !

Chapter Seven

The Noughties

I think carp fishing has changed drastically over the last few years. It is more noticeable to those of us that have fished that much longer as I think we have had more time in which to compare the changes. Originally I wasn't going to mention some of my feelings, but what is the point of writing a book if you can't be true to your gut instincts? It must be around ten years since the closed season was abolished and to be perfectly honest I didn't like the idea of it from the off. Not only do the carp not get a rest from the pressure but nor do the lakes. By that I mean the bankside vegetation and wildlife. For at least the last eight years or so I have read with interest the demise of numerous big carp from any number of high profile venues. Almost every time a big, well known carp has died there seems to be an air of mystery surrounding the death. By that I mean in almost all cases there has always been an excuse or something not quite definitive enough, like it was low oxygen levels, or because of the long cold winter - this has happened or that has happened. Or, well it was a very old fish. Has no one ever considered that stress may be killing these big carp? Stress is a massive killer of us humans and who is qualified to say categorically that stress isn't killing these big carp? Let's face it the pressure on big carp and the waters that hold them is relentless these days - it's 24/7 isn't it? Anglers that constantly target the biggest carp in the country are at it continuously. Carp fishing is big business and with that goes the commercial aspect, and publicity. Big carp are part and parcel of all that as they are the ones who are being used to promote products. I don't doubt for one minute that there will be those who accuse me of scaremongering. STRESS IN CARP? The bloke is stark raving mad! Just like they said all those years ago when I dared to say that I felt high levels of fish oils or fat content in a bait was detrimental to a carp's wellbeing and health. It wasn't until someone like Rod Hutchinson started to suggest that there was indeed an issue with high concentrations of fish oils in bait that the rest of the carp fishing fraternity took notice and indeed did something about it. Here is my theory: since the abolition of the closed season the pressure on a large percentage of waters has intensified no end. You can't hide the fact that the pressure on waters has been relentless. I can remember having a conversation with Peter Springate when we fished Horton. He had been watching some carp's reaction to baits lying on the lake bed and he said to me, "Do you know what? They look like they are shit scared of picking up a bait!" And that has to be well over seventeen years ago. Just recently I took part in a charity match where 28 guys fished 28 swims all weekend and guess what, the whole lake shut down, only two carp were caught all weekend. It was like the carp went into lock down! And the stock fish have only been in there for six years. Is it me or is that not alarming? Over the last twenty-five years I have fished some very highly pressured waters, but have noticed, more so since the abolition of the closed season, that things are definitely not right. How many big carp have died since the abolition of the closed season? I would hazard a guess that per water it is far more in that time than ever before. Forget the fish kills caused by stocking with illegal fish or infected fish as this was rife. I am talking about since the abolition of the closed season. I won't labour the point as I have said it but I, along with many others, have personally witnessed what we would call drastic changes in the carp's behaviour. What happened to all the major feeding periods before the winter sets in? Why do lakes shut down when the angling pressure builds up to a ridiculous point? Quite often on pressured waters once the weekend arrives very few fish get caught. I have personally turned up on a Sunday night to witness the carp's behaviour once all the lines from the weekend have been withdrawn. I am not alone in this, the change in the behaviour of carp is so evident for all to see and this has been going on for at least ten years. All that has happened over the last five years or so is that it has escalated; you can't tell me that is not an issue for concern? My suggestion? Reinstate the closed season!

Moving on, how do you deal with the very real fact that on these pressured waters it is becoming harder to fool the carp? Look at all the so-called modern day edges that are designed to supposedly give us an advantage over the carp. Fluorocarbon line, sinking leaders, vanishing anti-tangle tubing, see through leads, and anti-tangle tubing. Do these things really make a difference to our catches? Do they empty the lakes? Or are they more designed towards emptying our pockets? A very interesting question don't you think? I should know better but like a lot of you out there I too have been sucked into this fluorocarbon fetish. The all conquering vanishing line that is guaranteed to up your catch rate. Does it? I can't speak for any one else other than Tony Tappenden whom I fish with and have done so for as long as I can remember. We both came to the conclusion that it doesn't make the slightest bit of difference to your catch rate. It always makes me chuckle when you see a well known angler promoting the latest brand of fluorocarbon line and reveals how well he is doing using it. Well he would, wouldn't he, he is being paid to promote it! Call me a little cynical if you like but isn't that how it works?

Another old long-time mate of ours, Ted Bryant, who catches more than his fair share, uses normal line right through to his inline lead with no tubing at all and has done so for ages and he still catches big carp, and plenty of them. Personally I think that catching carp relatively consistently is more down to confidence and angling ability than all these new gadgets designed to enhance our results. Also how you

The three amigos

fish compared to what is going on around you I think is vitally important. On a lot of waters where the majority are chucking out as far as possible there will always be a case for fishing close in. Most of the time there is very little evidence to show that carp are in fact right under your feet, unless you keep your eyes open. Pressure has accounted for that situation. Carp have indeed learned to feed very close in as that is probably where a lot of bait gets dumped. You change your hook bait and where does the old one go? Usually in the margin. You fire out bait in a catapult and quite often a few baits overspill into the margins. When you pack up fishing, you may be in a hurry to get home to the wife and kids as you are being given a hard time by her indoors, what do you do? Sling the left over bait in the margins! On one water I was fishing, which for some time has been a very pressured water at times, I caught as many as five or six fish in a fourteen hour session and all within TEN yards of the bank. Obviously you can't hide the fact that you have caught fish, but you can hide the fact of where you caught them from. Quite often I would cast out say fifty yards then make it look like I am sinking the line, but in fact I would wind back the lead and bait to my chosen spot, DONK, down it would go and the job's done. On occasions after catching I would pack up and go home but return for a look round the next day when lo and behold someone is in the swim and their lines don't touch the water for twenty yards. You know that they know you caught in that swim. What they don't know is where you caught them from. It is always satisfying to know that they are fishing about forty to sixty yards past where the fish have been feeding. I know that is more than deceitful but so are some other anglers these days. Where I fish we call it the 'Kent Swerve'. Not wishing to upset anyone but I have never understood the mentality of some people who think all carp live at 160 yards range out in the lake, and I know one or two that do! I have fished at 130 yards on some lakes on occasions but that is when they are out there. It really is a case of fishing to the situation and circumstances don't you think? Carp fishing these days has become so unpredictable due to pressure etc that in order to try and give yourself half a fighting chance you have to try and be different. Occasionally you can do that with bait but more often than not it is doing something different that will make the difference. For as long as I can remember when someone is catching more than others on a lake it is usually down to something very simple that has made the difference, it can be rigs, type of bait, shape of bait, size of hooks, type of hook link material. Most of the time, successful methods are successful because they are the complete opposite to what most people are doing on that given lake at that time.I have always felt that it is 'Danger' by association, that's why carp get wary of a particular method and learn to avoid it or deal with it. In general most of my friends fish just overnight sessions so don't have the time for guesswork, it's all down to ability, and doing something different. More often than not when I go on a new water I will look at what is being done by most anglers and do my best to do exactly the opposite. On the water I am on at the moment, and hope to be on for many years to come, it soon became very apparent that there is a high turnover of anglers. By that I mean overnighters. The biggest worry is that on the odd occasions when I have done two nights together I managed to see a pattern going on. It happens with frightening regularity - a guy turns up in the swim, gets out the marker rod, finds a spot then spods a lot of bait to it and does the night. More often than not he blanks, then goes home. The next bloke comes in to the same swim and the whole process repeats itself. That worries me greatly, some would say at least there is bait going in that swim all the time to attract fish. Maybe, but I would rather have my baits as the only baits in that swim rather than three hundred of someone else's. On far too many occasions now I have watched where the fish come into the area, sometimes they might dip down and have a couple of baits, but more often than not they just pass through the swim and ignore the bait. It is no coincidence that over the last ten years all of my fish have been caught over very limited bait. By that I mean two bait stringers if 14mm or 16mm baits, or eight to ten size 10mm baits. On one water all my fish captures for the whole year were caught on that method. With more and more people using sticks, bags or netting, the more successful I have been in general in terms of carp on the bank. It's my honest opinion that if you have feeding carp in front of you, why on earth would you want to fire baits out over their heads? Not only does it spook them on pressured waters but adds to the baits in the area you are fishing, twenty baits in the swim means a 20/1 chance of a pick up, one hundred baits and its 100/1 chance, so on and so forth. I've watched blokes piling in kilo after kilo of bait and sitting on it for three or four days and still not get any action. I don't doubt that on occasions a huge bed of quality bait will indeed get you results if the fish have a big feed up. I haven't seen that situation where I have been fishing on more than the odd occasion throughout the year.

On another water I was fishing, the only way I could get consistent results was to fish with no more than two large handfuls of processed hemp with a single 10mm balanced hook bait fished over the top. Any more than that and no takes occurred. That wasn't worked out overnight - it took me a whole year of trying different things to get it right. Then the following year I caught consistently and the only time I blanked was when the conditions were rubbish or I wasn't on fish. I just think that on very, very pressured waters, and there are loads of them in the area I fish, that there is a very fine line between catching and not. On the water I am fishing at this time there are no consistencies in the fishing. It is just the odd fish being caught here and there, either on a single hook bait just chucked out any old how or on a single solid bag. But you don't learn anything from that do you? I would much rather know why I am catching or why I am not catching than just plod along on guesswork and chance. Once you have got your method working for you then you will definitely reap the rewards for much longer or until the carp suss you out! But if you don't fish with your eyes open then you learn sod all. I think your fishing is far more enjoyable and rewarding when you know why you are catching. Maybe a lot of anglers these days don't really care why they are catching as long as they are. Each to their own, eh?

One of the bullets . . . !

Angry looking, a huge bald patch, and the fish ain't much better

This one lived at 130 yards range . . .

Jim Gibbinson said to me . . . thats scale, fin and mouth perfect!

This one came from 130 yards - not my usual range!

Look at the length of that!

Chapter Eight

The Darenth Complex -
The Mental Squad, Lunatics &
Vagabonds, Every One!

W here do I begin with this one? I had dabbled a bit on the Darenth complex in the seventies but it just wasn't for me personally at that time and I don't know why. I think you either blend into a lake and become embroiled in it or you don't. If you don't, then go elsewhere. If you don't get that intimacy of where you fish then you are going to struggle. But circumstances were to change when in December 1991, I think, Gary Harrow and Dave Lawrence's son Rodney had just caught a hatful of carp from the Big Lake during a Friday to Sunday session. I honestly can't remember the exact amount but it may have been a dozen fish whilst field testing my new bait, the Factor 7. They had prebaited for approximately two weeks and it kicked in. It was such a special result that the *Angler's Mail* ran a whole page on the story. So it was to begin! Obviously at that time I was spending far more time developing baits, researching new products, tracking down and locating sources and bulk supplies of ingredients, additives, oils, flavours etc. In fact, so much so, I was struggling to get down the lake. I would be lucky to get a night in once a week or even once a fortnight. But during whatever time I could manage to fish I was meeting these hardened Darenth valley characters and anglers. Some of these blokes were clearly outstanding, very well informed and innovative anglers. I know that there were rumours flying about that some of these blokes were a bit thuggish and over the top - those rumours were usually put about by those who had to sit in silence and watch the Darenth boys stack the carp up like breeze blocks. Since time began there have always been the snipers and rumour mongers who slag off the successful because their own shortcomings don't allow them to be as successful as those who work at it. But I tell you what, give me those guys to fish with any day over some of the clowns I've come across in my time, that's for sure.

Some of the most inspired and secretive ideas, rigs, methods and set ups I have ever come across were born or invented on the banks of the Darenth complex, and by those blokes who fished there. I consider it a privilege to have known and to have fished alongside them. Amongst the Darenth crowd were a bunch of blokes, who to be fair were not quite all the ticket! If you know what I mean. They were known as the Mental Squad, quite an appropriate term really! But nevertheless very good, and caring anglers. I think the name / term or whatever you want to call it originated from the Streeter brothers, Melvin and Joe, who quite frankly were off the scale in terms of lunacy, especially Melvin, but what a great couple of blokes. I bumped into Joe only a couple of months ago (at the time of writing) and he is still just as crazy. Ha, ha, ha, luv it! Those guys accepted me as one of them, which was a nice touch as I guess I would have been considered old school to them even that

The Pallets swim Tip Lake.

The view from the dock!

far back, but nevertheless their company was exceptional. It soon became blatantly apparent that these blokes were very serious about their carp fishing; the care of those fish they fished for was paramount. As time went on I found myself drifting into a world of pure enjoyment in my fishing, occasionally there was the odd bit of agrro, but I was running a bait company now and soon realised it was part and parcel of that situation. By now my bait company had become established and was doing well. I was supplying bait to anglers all over the country, and the feedback I was getting was fantastic, although quite a few of those guys in the north of the country were rather keen to keep it quiet that they were using my baits. They were catching very well, and I guess they wanted to keep it quiet as it was mainly considered Hutchy and Nutrabaits territory up there. Although I would have liked the publicity, I realised it was their prerogative to keep it quiet. I would like to say at this point that I took great pride in the fact that even though I was writing every month for Carpworld and the odd other magazine, that not once did I mention that I ran my own bait company, nor did I plug any baits or products. I hated that side of things as anglers were being subjected to self plugging in articles at every opportunity to the point of complete boring saturation. I know many anglers who stopped buying monthly magazines because they were sick of it. I found the whole thing embarrassing and thought it was just a cheap shot . . .

I don't know where it came from, but I think it may have been Lee Jackson, who at the time was organising meetings for the Carp Society, who asked if it was possible to do a slide show based on the captures of the Mental Squad and my previous twenty years' fishing. I agreed to do with it along with Gary Harrow, who was mercilessly pushed forward by the others in the Mental Squad. We agreed to put as much humour into it as possible, mainly because there had been a group of guys a few years earlier who had put on a hugely successful slide show entitled the Chad Valley slide show. Not just that but we had seen a few slide shows put on by guys who probably took themselves a bit too seriously, and so we wanted to entertain far more than to say 'oh, look what we've caught'. This is always a bit dull really, so comedy was to be the main feature. I only have so much room for photos in this book but I will try and add as many of the photos we used to give you an idea of the humour we employed. It took so much planning, taking photos and arranging that it drove us more insane than we were already. We probably did more pictures at Cotton Farm than anywhere, mainly because it was much quieter than Darenth. When we finished everything I would like to think we did a good job of the humour side plus a lot of questions were asked afterwards by the audience. So I guess we pulled it off. I would have to say that I learned a hell of a lot by fishing at Darenth as there are an awful lot of very clever and innovative anglers here in Kent. I like to think that I have come up with some good ideas on rigs and set ups over the years, but without doubt some of the ideas I was shown during my time on there were indeed revolutionary. The Darenth complex could at times be very difficult, especially the Big Lake, so you really did have to work at it if you wanted to succeed in getting amongst the fish.

I can't remember how long I actually spent on the complex, not that long, maybe two or three years. To be perfectly honest the fishing, although fantastic, was just a bit too intense for me, I preferred to pop down and see the lads, see how they were doing, have a social and a good laugh. Because we had baited Cotton Farm, which was a darn sight quieter, I tended to go over there. I could get away from the rat race, chill out, put my feet up and enjoy it more. People don't seem to realise that if you run a bait company, then you are at it all the time from Monday to Friday and flat out making bait. The weekends always saw people coming to your house to pick up bait as they couldn't get to you in the week. When they turned up they wanted to talk endlessly about the subject of bait. That was my fault though, as I didn't have separate premises to run my business at normal times. Therefore I was inviting the inevitable. This is why I tended to go for the quieter waters to get some peace from it all. Cotton Farm was a very surreal place, the lake had been back filled and landscaped, dirty great boulders everywhere, and all the swims were covered in large stones of maybe two to three inches across. Then there were plants, and sprinklers everywhere that were all covered up by bark chippings. It was all topped off by pretty lights all over that lit the place up at night. It was like continuous daylight, very weird. The first night I fished I got down and decided on setting up just off the main swim on the far high bank as I couldn't handle the noise as you walked across the stones. It was like walking across Brighton beach, crunch, crunch, crunch, it was doing my head in. Anyway I set up my oval amongst the plants that formed the flower borders, and was so tired that I just crashed out once I had got the baits out. I must have drifted off into a deep sleep as the next thing I knew was I was soaking wet and there was a whooshing kind of sound, jets of water were bouncing off the under side of my oval and dropping back down over me . . . "fucccccccccccccckinhell," I shouted, I was completely drenched. It suddenly dawned on me that I had set up right on top of a poxy sprinkler. It was pure pandemonium trying to get all my gear out from underneath the brolly, my bedchair, sleeping bag, tackle, holdall-everything was drenched, including myself. I was soaked through to the skin . . . I stood there dripping wet but managed to start laughing and thanking my lucky stars that none of my mates were there to witness the scene. I would have been slaughtered left right and centre.

Other strange things happened to me at Cotton Farm when one night I had set up at the bottom of the steps on the high bank. It was a bit tricky as you had to carry all your gear down about sixty odd steps down to the water's edge where there was a small platform to put your bedchair on and lean your brolly over you to one side. I had got my rods out and settled in and after a short time obviously nodded off. At some point in the early hours, maybe 2.00am or thereabouts, I was awoken by the sound of voices. Straight away I went for the mallet and a bankstick in case it was tackle thieves. I was trapped at the bottom of a set of steps with no way of escape other than to dive in the oggin. I looked up and was really freaked out by the sight of two bright white T-shirts and nothing else coming down the steps towards me. By the time they were halfway down the steps it was getting weirder by the minute as it suddenly dawned on me that apart from the T-shirts they were both stark bollock naked. Now if the bird had been halfway sensible, I would never have minded but it was not a pretty sight. I can tell you, all her under carriage sticking out like a docker's hook! Jesus . . . I didn't deserve that! And the geezer wasn't much better - another half inch shorter and it would have been countersunk! I am now thinking what the hell these two were doing walking halfway around the lake naked at 2 o'clock in the morning. Do you know what made it worse? They just stared at me. "Alright, you two, how's things," I said, "are you lost or something?" Not a murmur came back, the hairs on the back of my neck stood up and visions of 'The Deliverance' came before my eyes - "I'm gonna make you squeal boy!" Then all of a sudden they just turned around and walked back up the steps and vanished. Needless to say I gave it ten minutes, packed my gear up and got out of there as fast as my barrow would carry me. I can't remember who I spoke to the next day but when I explained what had happened they said that apparently there used to be a mental hospital not far away from the lake, which had been shut down, and these two were outpatients or something and they just kept coming back to the lake. Needless to say I never did another night on there for at least eight years. I think about the time Lee Jackson took over the running of the syndicate and that was a right result for me as I landed the big common at 40lb 12oz on my third trip back on the venue. Maybe there was some justice done after all.

I ended up going back on the Darenth for the winter, as fish were coming out and ended the season with a couple of perfect linears that were not supposed to exist. Some anglers were putting it around that all the Darenth carp were a mess with torn mouths and damaged fins. I wonder how many Darenth carp those people caught to assume that, eh ? Not a lot, I am thinking. By now I had started to think about fishing the Larkfield complex. I had fished the Johnson's complex on and off since 1970 but I had never even considered Larkfield No 2. Nor had I even really looked at it. I knew my old mucker Steve Edwards had fished it. He told me that it wasn't easy but, if you got into it, and you really took notice of what the fish did, he said I would catch. But you had to eat, sleep, and breath Larkfield, and really get into it. Which did indeed prove to be the case . . .

One from the mud . . .

Terry releasing Small Head

Graham Hackett with the Brown Fish, Tip Lake

Big Lake mirror

Dave Lawrence . . . he really knows his stuff

Chapter Nine

Sutton-at-Hone

I first fished Sutton way back in the late seventies. I believe, and hope I am right when I say that HAS Fisheries (Hall's Angling Scheme) controlled the water at that time. I first fished it with a couple of mates from Bromley, Norman (Nobby) Gatsell and John (Piggy) Bellini. I knew my old lifetime best mate Steve Edwards, Terry (Gaggy) Gauge plus Colin Cameron and John Kemp, were also fishing there. It was relatively unknown at the time, under normal circumstances I would have been fishing in the bait group with them but ironically I had just committed the cardinal sin. I had been fishing with Colin Cameron and John Kemp who I had grown up with on the council estate on Bromley Common, and had been in the secret sect of the Wilton bait group for quite a few years and sworn to secrecy. But I had also been best mates with John and Colin who obviously were not on Fred's bait. This put me in a very difficult predicament and being young and somewhat naïve I gave in to their constant interrogation over the bait I was using. Eventually I told them that we were using lemon flavouring as the label . . . well all hell broke loose. Anyone would think I had just broken the secret service code. I was banished to the outskirts of the Kent underworld like a leper of the worse proportions. I just thought, "Well f*** you lot, I will sort my own bait out." The truth is that it probably did me a big favour as I now had to work it all out for myself. The irony of it is that Colin and John ended up fishing with Steve and had access to the bait anyway. Ha, ha, ha, what a load of old b*******s this carp fishing lark is. Anyway after about six months or so they had brought me back from Coventry and started talking to me again. They were on the milk proteins and John, Norman and I were on the ground up malt shreddies special with Langdale's wild cherry flavouring. We were catching loads of carp from Sutton and it was a constant wind up over whose bait was best.

Another ironic thing happened when I ended up catching what was at the time the biggest common in Sutton - a capture that would repeat itself many years later (no change there then). Eventually I lost interest in the place because it was getting so busy, much too busy for my liking, so I went off and started fishing a complex near Sevenoaks. Fast forward to about 1994/5 when Steve Edwards had landed the job of area coordinator for Leisure Sport Angling and I had just started fishing Larkfield No2 with Ted Bryan and Graham Hackett. It was a pretty lawless place back then, ironically that is what it has turned back into now. I was as usual moaning to Steve about the place and as it was also under the Leisure Sport Angling banner he turned to me and said, "Don't moan, Happy, sort the gaff out yourself, I will make you head bailiff." He squared it with Ian Welch and we were

Rewind to the seventies . . . I am convinced it's the same fish as the one of 38lb 12oz

up and running. I appointed twelve bailiffs and we started to improve the Larkfield complex. New swims were built and I take pride in the fact that between us and the local lads we transformed the lakes into a fantastic venue. Anyway, with the head bailiff's job on Larky came a free ticket for LAS as a bonus.

To be perfectly honest I wasn't much interested in Sutton, as I knew that most of the time you were fishing against other anglers rather than for than the carp. Sutton had a habit of being very busy. With no night fishing (cough, cough, Tappy) it was damn hard work to fish it seriously if your time was limited. I would turn up to fish after work about 7 o'clock in the evening on a Friday, get the rods out then you were out of the gate at 10.30pm, or so, then off to the pub, get a few pints down your neck, then crash out in the car. Set the alarm for 3.00am, and back on the gate for the draw at whatever ungodly hour we were allowed in at. Was it 3.30am? Then fish till about 11.00pm, in my case, pack up and go home shattered. I had a young family back then so had daddy's duties to perform. Hardly conducive to catching with any regularity but I did OK for a part timer. The other thing was I had my head well and truly into Larkfield so I think I treated my time on Sutton as a social with the lads I liked a lot who, like me, enjoyed a social and a wind up.

Sutton mirror late 70s

Derek Linstead, Tappy , Steve Edwards, George Mills, Keith Pepper, Keith Sullivan, 'Dodgy' Denholm, Joe Jarman, Paul Owen, John Carver, Terry the boxer, Gary the worm, Ian McMillan, Graham East, Micky Fisher, Ian Tester, John Elmer - the list goes on and on. I know for certain I have forgotten a few, sorry for that, but I am trying to write a book here.

I remember meeting Terry Hearn there when he was in the Pipes, I think, and I was in the Wide. About twenty yards out in front of us were the carp doing their usual trick of boshing all over the place, fizzing up, tearing up the bottom and doing everything except getting caught. They were crashing all over Terry's rods and mine, but as usual nothing, not even the odd liner. The water between us resembled a boiling cauldron. I'll never forget, he came round for a chat as obviously the fish were in front of both of us and looked at me and said, "Where I usually fish, if they were doing this on my lake I would have had three by now." I looked at him and trying not to smile I said, "Welcome to Sutton, mate!"

I have mixed feelings about Sutton, some good some bad, but mostly good, I can remember creeping up to the front of the back pads swim and peering over the edge as the fish got in so close there. On this occasion there were about five

I'm in again . . . Gaggy waits with the net . . .

fish literally twelve inches off the bank and I recognised one of them as the Fully
Scaled. I carefully crept back on all fours to get my rod, manoeuvred back to the
spot and very slowly lowered my bait down from the tip being so careful not to
spook the fish - once in place I lay there just breaking up a couple of baits and
flicking the tiny bits out amongst the spot where my hookbait was. I sat there
watching as the tails wafted over the spot and small vortices hit the surface as the
fish searched out the tiny bits of bait. I had to hold my heart to stop the thumping
from travelling through the ground and spooking the fish as I knew I was in with
a major shout of catching the Fully Scaled when all of a sudden whooooooooosh
a dirty great lead landed six feet from the bank . . . sperlosh! All hell broke loose
and there were bow waves everywhere that left my swim rocking. The pads were
swaying back and forwards. Jesus I was fuming . . . I got to my feet and shouted,
"You're having a f*****g laugh ain't you mate!" He had cast all the way over from
the Double Willow swim some forty poxy yards away. "Sorry mate, I didn't see you
there!" "That's the f*****g idea you clown I retorted." That was the only thing I
disliked really about Sutton was the handful of blokes who had no idea of fishing
etiquette. They could ruin your chances of a fish just by the way they fished.

The good side of Sutton however was the social side, how we all loved the

Sound & Round dos, the presentations, the absolute slaughtering you got in front of everyone. No one was exempt from the wrath of Millsy, Boza, or Jarman. Or even the Worm. If you were in the line of fire, there was no mercy. Poor old Tappy had spent about eight months in agony as he had loads of work done on his shattered leg. Some little old dear had pulled out in front of him as he went down the road on his bike and messed his leg up big time. Anyway he was hobbling about with a stainless steel cage wrapped round his leg that was a work of art that Lockie just could have made. But that didn't stop the boys from ripping into him. I think it was Millsy who threw a bag of nuts and bolts at him saying, "Here you go Tappy, have some spare parts just to be on the safe side." Or words to that effect. I was given a load of round pike bungs to shove up my backside as I had said earlier in the year after the lead in my swim incident that I would not fish Sutton again as long as I had a hole in my a***. Well I was back on there and had to pay for my remark. Then there was the Tampax Cup for whoever had fished like a c*** all year. I will let you work that one out for yourself; someone was presented with what was described as Richard Walker's ashes. Lee Jackson got slaughtered, Lockie was supposed to turn up and was in for a mouthful, but fortunately for him he never arrived. The list goes on and on, no one was spared, the bigger your profile in carp fishing the further you had to fall. I can honestly say that on every single occasion I attended a Sound & Round meeting I went home absolutely hammered, with rib cage damage and jaw ache from the laughing non stop all evening. I've had some fun in my time, leg pulling, stroke pulling, mickeytaking, you name it but nothing compares to the outrageous behaviour of that crew at the meetings.

The last meeting of the Sound & Round crew could never be bettered or equalled. Even more so that Steve and George are no longer with us. Sutton was a breeding ground for fun filled events to enjoy.

One winter me, Tappy and Lovejoy (Derek Linstead) were sitting in the Twins swim and we were mucking about as usual talking nonsense when Tappy rebaited and said to me, "Here Happy, what do you think of this rig then?" It was pitch black but Tappy had his head torch on so I leant over to examine his rig that was dangling in front of my face. I then slipped on something and was off balance for a second and as I was falling forward I could see Tappy's hook heading towards my eye so I turned my head and felt a pop. It was the sound of his wide gape hook catching my nostril and the pop was the noise made as the barb went through the skin of my nose from the inside to the outside. "That hurt," I said, as I was left hanging on Tappy's rig with his boilie poking out of my inner nostril. All I could see was Tappy's light in my eyes. I was fumbling about in the dark for his line

'Mugger' Mills, he could make them laugh. What a character!

so as to grab it and stop him from pulling my nose off my face with his rod ". . . aaaaarrrrggggghhh . . . keep still," I shouted.By now the pair of them were wetting themselves and the more they laughed the more his rod moved and the more pain I was getting . . . anyone one else who was fishing must have thought we were mad. Eventually out came the wire cutters and they pulled the hook far enough through my nose to cut off the barb, then pull out the rest of the hook from my nostril. Many a night I have been ridiculed by those two for that night and now I am writing my book they both say we should have taken a picture of it that night. Yeah, right!

If I am totally honest, there was an element that I didn't like about Sutton and that was some of the guys on there had condemned Ken Rowley for fishing in the lilies which were, what, no more than twenty feet across. They had accused him of snag fishing if you please. The fact of the matter is Ken was catching fish on floater cake freelined into the pads, and regularly too. They made some cock and bull story up about him damaging fish's mouths by fishing there. What a load of cobblers. Ken, Steve and I had been brought up fishing Keston where the lilies were at times forty yards wide not twenty bloody feet and not once did we damage a fish's mouth. The fact was that they didn't like Ken catching fish - plain and simple. Snag fishing . . . they would have run a mile if confronted with fishing Keston.

The strangest thing was that during my brief return to Sutton I never caught a mirror; every fish I caught was a common. I am not complaining because I managed to catch one of the biggest commons in there at that time at weight of 38lb 12oz. The fish had not been caught for well over a year, if my memory serves me, or maybe about fifteen or sixteen months. Ironically I reckon it was exactly the same fish that I caught back in the seventies, which again was i think one of the biggest commons in there at the time On that morning Steve and I had walked on together from the gate and walked up the fence bank. We stopped on the point and we could hear the odd fish crashing out some thirty yards in the darkness. Steve said, "This will do for me, Happy." So I replied, "OK mate, I will have a look in the Hole swim." I would then be parallel to where we had heard the fish crash. I went round and stood in the Hole and a fish stuck its head out at thirty yards from me. This was far enough away from Steve for me not to interfere with where he was casting. At the time I was using three inch long hairs on light running leads and small backleads. I cast both rods into the darkness where the fish had crashed and fired out about a dozen baits over both rods. Once I sorted the rest of the tackle out I made a cup of coffee and sat back to take in the atmosphere. It wasn't long before I was getting liners so I knew I was on fish and I could hear Steve's buzzers going off. Obviously we were both on a lot of fish, my right-hand indicator kept pulling up and setting off the buzzer as I squinted in the half light of the approaching dawn. I was sure the tip of my rod was just bouncing slightly. I knew these Sutton fish were very tricky, and as I was contemplating hitting it Steve had a one noter . . . get in my son I thought. Then my rod certainly bounced, that fish was definitely trying to get off. I wound down and pulled up to the back lead from the very deep margin in front of me and sure enough something out there was plodding about. I love plodding fish, more often than not they are big fish. Steve and I were playing fish at the same time, not exactly a rare occurrence. By now I could see Steve netting his fish as the sky was welcoming the dawn, but I had a battle on my hands as the fish I was attached to wasn't having any of it. Deep lunges all the time, it would just swim off parallel to the brambles staying deep. Eventually Steve came round as did Keith Sullivan to see what the commotion was . . . "Come on Happy you are making a meal of that my son," said Steve, "I've landed my fish, taken pictures, put it back and you are still playing yours." I replied, "That, my son is because this is a whacker!" The closer to the bank I got the fish the bigger the swirls and by now I could see Keith and Steve looking at each other in that knowing fashion. They knew it was a lump too, so the barracking stopped and the more serious matter of netting it was attended to. Anyway it ended up in the net and a few choice words were hurled in my direction once they saw how big it was. But nonetheless they were happy for me. Now strangely enough my biggest common, which I caught back in the late seventies from Sutton, I am convinced is exactly the same fish. Have a look for yourself and see what you think. Some things in carp fishing are just pre-ordained I think and somewhat ironic. Sutton holds some stunning fish, no question about that, and I met some great blokes on there, and very good anglers who took their fishing seriously. Some of them still fish there today and like Steve they just love the place. All of them quite clearly see something in the place that I never did. It never really got under my skin like it did others. The sad thing is that right now its future, along with all the other waters Cemex Angling controls, is up in the air and for sale. This is of some concern, as the history of these waters is threatened by the instability of this country's financial situation. I sincerely hope they don't end up like Johnson's Snag Lake, as a set of footings for a housing project.

... the first fish on my return to Sutton

Part of a rare Sutton brace from the Wide ...

Tappy . . . with one of his many Sutton fish

Not captured for 18 months but I put her on the bank. Now named Happy's Common, 38lb 12oz

Another common, Sound & Round!

Chapter Ten

Larkfield - Home of the Brave

Where oh where could I possibly start with Larkfield? I had known about Larkfield for donkey's years, ever since I walked onto the Johnson complex I knew it existed, but to this day I still can't work out why I hadn't fished it. It never even entered my head, I was more interested in the Road and Island Lake and the Snag Lake really and the Ocean. I had been fishing Barden Park with my two close mates, Graham Hackett and Ted Bryan, but I think we had had enough of the place. The only forty in there had been dropped on the floor by someone and obviously died. We had already caught loads out of there, so a move was on the cards. At that time Leisure Sport had the control of the fishing rights so we obtained a ticket and went down for a have-a-look session. We set up in a line along the bottom half of the lake from the willows to the back point which is on the railway bank. It was early April I believe and bloody cold. We did the usual thing of having a social. There wasn't a soul on the lake, dawn came and out in front of us were carp crashing one after the other. Well, we said, we are in the right place. After about three hours of watching those fish crash all over us it became evident that these Larky carp were not going to be a pushover. I did my usual trick of saying . . . "It's all a matter of rigs and converting a pick up into a take!" Ted and Graham just laughed at me; they know what I am like for changing rigs until I get a take. I refuse to be beaten by a fish! I threw the kitchen sink at those fish, every single trick I had in the book. I did eventually get a half hearted take which I struck, whatever it was only stayed on for about thirty seconds then fell off, but food for thought. Quite clearly we were going to need to get a bait established, and think over a plan of attack.

Steve Edwards had already given me lots of information about the place, but he did say to me that, "Those Larky carp love a bit of quality bait, but if you want to catch them, you need to get into the lake, the fish and the surroundings. You have to eat, sleep and breathe it all in." He said it won't be easy . . . we had been using the LT94 in our bait for about three or four years and the results had spoken for themselves, so bait was not an issue. Steve Edwards had located the LT94 herring meal and Peter Springate and Steve had come up with a formulation for the bait. Peter was field testing it during the winter on Fork Pond and was emptying the place, but they couldn't obtain the LT94 in bulk. That's where I came in. I managed to track down the depot where it was coming into the country and arranged to buy it by the ton. It was agreed that the mix would be made up by Bob Baker at Richworth under the banner of the 'Low Fat Ultra Mix'. This was fantastic, the mix was a very easy to roll mix so Bob had no problem putting it through his rollers, so we were sorted. We started introducing the bait and to be perfectly honest I can't

Under the Willows, Johnsons Railway Lake circa 1980

remember what flavour we used when we first started putting it in, but I wasn't confident. I don't know why, normally I don't have a problem with that side of my fishing but we had made a half hearted decision, and it wasn't right. I don't know who suggested it but I had received a large sample of a crayfish flavour that I said we could take 10ml of this flavour and throw it in a two kilo bag of frozen bait and as it thawed the flavour would be drawn into the frozen bait, and it would mask whatever was in there. This we did. As I recall, it worked straight away and I think Ted was the first one to catch on the modified bait. It was instant, so we asked Bob Baker to make us some more bait but with the new crayfish flavour. Slowly but surely we introduced the bait all over the lake, not piling it in, but a few handfuls in every spot we thought the carp would visit at some point during a twenty-four hour period. Quiet bays, areas of rushes, marginal areas that you just couldn't put a hook bait to; there wasn't a place on that lake where the carp swam that they wouldn't find a handful or two of bait. You could do that back then. I don't think you can now without upsetting other blokes on the lake. There is no doubt in my mind that a handful of bait in the right place will have a huge advantage over ten kilos in the wrong place.

Anyway that first season was OK but not what I would call a success. It wasn't because the bait failed to work but how we were fishing. We had been used to Barden where you found fish, put out bait and caught them, plain and simple. But this was different - this was Larkfield. One major advantage occurred the next year. Up until that point I had been using Big Game line in a kind of sandy colour. We were using it because it was strong and reliable, as Larkfield is full of savage gravel bars. You can cast over one of the bars, which has, say, three to six feet of water on top of it but then it might drop down to twelve feet on the far side of the bar, and land on a shelf. If a carp picks you up and goes left or right you can get cut off just like that! So you needed a strong line, but I was never really happy with the colour of it. I reckoned the fish could see it all the time as it was like barge rope. I can't remember who it was who mentioned another line, it was either Rocky or Smudge - I think it was Rocky who for some reason mentioned a line called Silver Thread or something like that. It was, and is, the best line I have ever used beyond any shadow of a doubt. It is almost invisible in water, the 14lb breaking strain is very strong and abrasion resistant - you could pull trees over with it. It's a bit here and there when new, but once it has straightened and bedded in it's brilliant. Give me that over any line on the market today and I mean that sincerely. We used to buy it in 3000 yard spools but it's just more difficult to get in bulk spools these days. I think you can only get it now in 200 yard spools. Anyway . . . that line lifted my catch rate through the roof when my second season saw me land eighteen fish. I was well made up with that, bearing in mind that I only used to fish a fourteen hour overnight session on a Saturday night, once a week, and that wasn't every week. I think that year Ted caught 63 carp in the year, but he was fishing four or five nights in the week. I guess I was doing rather well for the time I put in. By now Rocky was on the bait, so was my old mucker Tony Tappenden. I can't actually remember the exact number, but I am guessing there were about six or seven of us on the bait now, and we were indeed having it off. Just remember this was Larkfield with a reputation for being hard. So, eighteen fish in a season to me was having it off big time. There were those who were really struggling - one bloke I know fished Larky for three seasons before catching his first carp. It's OK Mr Gadget I won't mention your name, eh Gary . . . ha, ha, ha. Bless you mate, more power to your elbow for sticking it out.

By now my old mate Steve Edwards had taken over the area coordinator job and the running of Leisure Sport Sutton, and had asked me to take on the job of head bailiff of Larkfield - which I gladly did. By now I had fallen under the spell of Larkfield and had grown to love the place. It really was a special water with very special carp, outrageously difficult to catch at times. Sometimes, like other waters, it gave up its treasures in a fashion that looked easy, but then it could turn on you and make you suffer for your arrogance. With the help of all the bailiffs and the local anglers, between us we slowly built Larkfield up and got it to a state of excellence that it hadn't been in before. All of the swims were maintained, reinforced, all the pathways were cut back so the local residents could walk the complex with ease and safety. I even persuaded Ian Welch to allow a boat on the venue so any fish snagged in the notoriously dense weed, which was at times a nightmare, could be landed safely. I was at last happy that between us all we had produced an incredibly respectful fishery. By now the locals had amassed a book of pictures of the Larkfield carp which they called the Larky Bible. The preservation of those fish was paramount. I can honestly say that of all the waters I have fished in the last forty-seven years, Larkfield was the only water alongside Keston that I have ever felt an affinity with. There were things I had seen carp do in Larky that I have never seen elsewhere. There were carp in Larkfield that hadn't been out in about eight years, I believe that to be true, loads of others felt the same.

There was one mirror, that at least six of us had seen, that was around upper thirty, maybe scraping 40lb. A thick-set fish with a deep body and smallish head. The distinguishing marks were two large scales on the flank in line with the lateral line, like an x in the middle of the flank, so it was unmistakable. I desperately

Johnson's Snag Lake - locked up solid

wanted to catch that fish so badly. I had seen it mostly just off the long island that is right at the end. So, I hatched a plan to bait up the spot where I had seen it most, which was close to the island. At that point it was quite deep and very silty with the sort of oozing black muck you really don't want to put a bait in. You never even got a drop-off in that area, but only about twelve feet out was a small bar that came off the bottom with maybe four feet of water on top of it. It ran for about twelve feet, parallel to the bank, before falling away back into nine feet then fifteen yards away came back up to within six inches of the surface. The only problem was there was a large bush growing on the top of the bar which people used to cast to from Paul's Point some sixty yards away. The top of the bar, or at least the side of it, would be where I would target the fish. I had seen the fish time and time again feeding on the side of the bar just before the sand and gravel met the silt and I would sit mesmerised as the fish would tear up the bottom. It threw sand and silt into the water medium as it snorted away along the bottom like a huge angry pig troughing away at the natural food and sending clouds of debris up in the air that turned the water a sandy colour. It was that big you could have thrown a saddle on the bugger and ridden it around the margins. The problem was that I didn't want anyone to know I was fishing the island so if I was going to bait up, it had to be after dark and done very quietly. Another problem was it was a nightmare to get out to the island in the daylight hours, let alone the bloody darkness. It was a fifty yard hike through rushes and water that could be three feet deep at times, so it was waders and fully clothed or get bitten to death by the mossies that lived in the rushes at night. It wasn't even a straight walk, but a winding, twisting wade through stinking silty water. Once you got to the island you then had to ease yourself onto the end and slide into a position to bait up. I made up a load of flat baits that I could just flick out to the bar so they wouldn't make a plopping sound otherwise the game would have been up! This was the easy part.When I fished, I had to get my tackle out to the island - it was hard enough just getting yourself out there let alone getting your tackle out as well. Anyone who knows me knows that for years I have used a small inflatable boat as my unhooking mat. Scruffy Bob made me a heavy duty cover that had a soft material top so any decent fish I caught could sit in there, well supported and safe from harm.

Well, I had to cut right back on the tackle and then put all my gear in the unhooking boat/mat and drag it behind me through the rushes out to the island. Raving bloody mad! I had baited for about three weeks and had seen the pig show in that area time and time again as I watched. If it was quiet on the lake during the day, I would sit out there amongst the trees watching carp feed on the baited bar. The Pig would at some point show. The particular night I went to do my first session on there everything was prepared ready. I had got a new set of Delkims with a remote from Del Romang so that any takes I got could not be heard all around the lake and give away that I was on the island. I waited until about eleven o'clock then made my way across to the island through the mossie infested rushes. Once there both the rods were underarm cast to the top of the bar and I then flicked out about twenty flat paste bait shapes. The traps were set. I turned the Delkim remote right down to a whisper and then felt knackered from the walk across and the nervous anticipation. I gazed out into the half light and as if on cue the Pig launched itself up out of the water and I just stared in disbelief as it came out side on. Jesus it looked huge in the half light and it just slipped back in to the water with hardly a sound. The ripples from its re-entry lapped up against the island and there was no doubt whatsoever what fish it was - it was too big a framed fish to be anything else. I don't know when, but at some point I must have crashed out as the next thing I remember was thinking, "What's that light I can see?" A bright red light! At first I thought I was in Soho, but then it was clear . . . it was the red light of my Delkim and the sound of the baitrunner burning itself out as whatever was on the end was motoring big time! Like a plank I had turned down

Larkfield No 2 mean and moody

Oscars, under the rod tips was best!

The back bay, Johnsons Snag Lake

the remote on the Delkims so much that I couldn't hear a thing . . . what a plank! I picked up the rod and as I pulled into the fish it just flattened out the rod . . . zzzzzzzzzzzzzzzzzzzzzzzzzzzz . . . the baitrunner was singing its morbid tune as the fish headed for the sanctuary of the dense rushes of Ted's Hole. Then in no time a huge crash as the fish found its sanctuary and all had gone solid with just the odd knock on the rod top as Mr Carp tried to push its snout further into the rushes. I was furious with myself for turning down the Delkim so low - what a tosser, Sometimes being too secretive can cost you big time. I held onto the rod to keep pressure on the fish as dawn broke with the mist slowly rising from the lake like some scene from a horror movie. What do I do now? I had no choice. I knew Rocky was over on the Railway and had a boat with him, so I put the rod down in the rest and waded over to the causeway between Larky and the Railway to get Rocky's boat. He helped me carry it across and we manoeuvred across to the rushes where the line went in and there it was . . . no not the fish but my hook, a Drennen Specialist, gleaming in the new morning sunlight. Obviously the fish had transferred the hook into the rush stem . . . (how do they do that?) and my secret was blown. Was it the fish I was after? I don't know, who would? How can you tell? But I have to say I do in my heart think it was the Pig. Shortly after that others went and fished on the island. The only trouble was they went and put up a frigging bivvy on the island, banged in the banksticks and would cast out the fifteen yards to the main bar that runs parallel to the island. This not only spooked any fish that moved along that bar but they were also casting about eleven yards past the best feature in the area. I can only shake my head . . . but isn't that modern day carp fishing? I have to say that I probably learnt more from Larkfield than fishing anywhere else, what with the clarity of the water and the wariness of those carp. I can say that honestly from what I saw and the reactions of those carp towards rigs, baits etc. Very few carp I saw fed in the same manner. All my efforts were concentrated in the margins, obviously because if I saw what they did in the margins, I could then deal with the problem of fooling the carp. I would feel far more confident in casting to one of the many features in the lake in the knowledge that I would at least know if one of those carp picked up my hookbait. I would then be in with a chance of tricking it. As an example, one of my mates, Andy Davies, who was on the bait, had been down for a day and a night and was fishing one of the Bottleneck swims. He had put out a couple of kilos of bait and had carp showing over his baited area but with only the odd pull now and again. I said to him, "It's your rigs Andy, they've sussed you out mate." He gave me that old fashioned look . . . "No, honestly mate show me your rigs." He wound in a twelve

inch hooklink and a standard type of lead clip set up. "Have you tried short
hooklinks yet?" I asked. "No not yet." I gave him a couple of my rigs - the run rig
set up with a three inch hooklink. I explained that I'd had good results on that set
up and it was fooling the fish. He agreed to try them out, even though I don't think
he was sure about such a short hooklink. I explained that it wasn't a short hooklink
as the set up had a backstop five inches away that effectively makes it an eight inch
hooklink, yes? Variable? I am not so sure he got it at first, but he did later as he
caught his first two Larkfield carp that afternoon. I am not saying that I am any
better an angler than Andy, but what I was doing was different. Even Ted Bryan
would look at me as I was casting out a rig with a nylon hooklink, a two and a half
inch 1lb 10 oz nylon hair and say, "I can't believe you are chucking that out in the
lake," but it was working, it's all about doing something different in my opinion.
Larkfield was getting harder as the seasons wore on and especially as I was fishing
Saturday nights only. By the time I got there it was packed, but you have to use that
as an advantage, not a disadvantage. It was pretty much the same scenario every
weekend come Friday afternoon the lake would fill up, anglers usually went into
the main swims either for a social, or so they could cast to quite an expanse of
water in front of them. Because they would be doing the weekend they would
bring the big bivvies with them, so what happened on a Friday, it would be marker
floats all over the gaff, spod, spod, spod, all afternoon trying to get the jump on
everyone else. This resulted in the tricky Larky carp making their way into all the
quiet bays, rush areas, small islands, any little area that was quiet and free from
marker floats and spods. Now, it just so happened that most of the swims, if you
could call them that, were so small in those areas that you could only just get an
umbrella in them. As head bailiff I made sure that small swims remained small.
Those areas were a gift as far as I was concerned. I never used more than two rods
in those areas and I also was aware that the carp already knew the bait. A one bait
stringer was all that was required in that situation. As my mate Tony Tappenden
always says . . . I want to catch 'em not feed 'em! I may fire out three or four baits
in the area but that was it. I already knew that swim after swim was crammed full
of bait and because the fish were spooked anyway by the disturbance, I needed to
be so quiet and careful. That particular season I managed to catch virtually every
Saturday night. On two occasions I caught braces - now you may be thinking that
I am being big headed here but that's not the case. Yes, I was fishing effectively but
a major factor in catching was that Rocky and Ted were full timers and were doing
at least four days a week. When I got down they would fill me in as to the
whereabouts of the bulk of the fish. Without question that was a huge part in me

catching. I owe them both a huge debt of gratitude for that. Larkfield carp could move in an instant. When we first went on there most of the carp would shoal up, but after a couple of highly pressured seasons it was evident that the carp were breaking up into much smaller groups. To give you an idea of how they could move, you could sit on the high bank on a strong south westerly and watch them porpoise down the lake. They went through the Bottleneck swims and onto the first, second, and third bars ending up crashing on the ends of the bars thirty yards from the high bank. Time and time again you could carefully cast a single hookbait at them using just an ounce and a quarter lead, and the next thing you would watch them porpoise back up the lake. There they would end up milling around the rushes up the top end . . . unbelievable. I don't know, but I would hazard a guess that Larky two is about three quarters of a mile long at least and those carp could go from end to end in no more than say ten minutes max. That alone made the place very difficult; sometimes you had the situation where the fish would literally stack up in front of the Motorbike swim, approximately half way down the lake just before the Bottleneck swims. They could sit there for a day or so then usually under the cover of darkness the fish would decide to push on through. It drove you nuts, liner after liner liner as they moved on down the lake. Most of the smart guys would pack up once that started and move down the lake to the second Bottleneck swim or the Elders or the Post swim and prepare for the oncoming carp! It all depended where they went. If they cut across the lake they could end up in front of the Willows and it was all a case of luck of the draw really. As I mentioned earlier, when you watched the fish in Larkfield feed you knew that to sort them out you would need to be very open minded on your outlook to rigs.

I tried all sorts and I remember reading about how Alan Taylor, an exceptional angler from around Bedford way, was having it off using four or five ounce leads where he was fishing. I knew Alan as he too was a BCSG member and back then we all used to contribute to the magazine, The Carp. The rotary letters, opening up about rigs and set ups etc and I did try and use the heavy lead set ups in the margins of the island. I tried large hooks, small hooks, short hooklinks, long hooklinks, nylon hooklinks, braided hooklinks, you name it I tried it. Not one single fish did I put on the bank with that approach. One evening I placed a bait on a four ounce lead in a clear patch surrounded by soft algae and Canadian pond weed. During the night I had a single bleep on the Delkim but as it was quite windy I put it down to the ripple on the water. In the morning with the sun cutting through the crystal clear water I peered down and saw a sight I dreaded. I wound up the line to my lead and it had been moved two feet from off the clear gravel shelf and dumped two feet away in amongst the algae and weed to the left of the spot. I never used a heavy lead set up again other than for casting at range on other lakes. It's all too final for me personally. What works on one lake for one angler is definitely not necessarily the answer to fishing on another lake in a completely different set of circumstances. There are quite a lot of anglers who believe that it is the lead that hooks the fish. Well all I can say is that for at least ten years I have never used a lead heavier than two ounces, and ninety percent of that time I have only used an ounce and a quarter lead. It's all about personal confidence. For myself, I think it has far more to do with how a fish ejects the bait. If your bait and hook separate on ejection and you are using very sharp hooks, then in my opinion the minute that carp is pricked it's game over on a running set up. That's another reason why I won't use a lead clip. It's all far too samey. On a running set-up or with a back stop I get the same take every time, the line tightens and the fish, is on the rod tip. It's goodnight nurse for me! If it's all down to the lead hooking the fish then why have I caught so many fish on a float? Where is the lead there then? Larkfield taught me so many things and fishing with heavy leads wasn't one of them! In my humble opinion a lead, regardless of weight, is just a vehicle for putting your hookbait where you want to get it. I have fished at 130 yards range and the lead did the job to get me to the feature I wanted to be on, but the biggest feature in the lake is the biggest bar in the lake and that is the marginal shelf, and you really don't need a 5oz lead to fish that!

It was at about this time that I met Tony (Tappy) Tappenden, who unbeknown to me at the time would become a best friend and fishing companion for life. He is a friend of Ted Bryant and had been for years and I remember that I had met him before somewhere as we had fished the same waters. Plus, he had already met my lifelong friend Steve Edwards up at Crystal Palace Park, where I had also fished. I think our paths had crossed up there. In the winter Ken Rowley, Steve and I fished the Palace for the pike. Tony had not been on Larkfield very long but was catching almost from the off. In fact 'Scaley' was one of the first fish he caught, (spawny git) says he who has had more than his fair share of good fortune. It wasn't long before we had ourselves a formidable force on Larkfield. Myself, Ted, Tappy, Rocky, Mad Steve, Bernie, Graham Hackett, Andy Davies, Nigel Kemp. Sorry if I have forgotten anyone else. It would be fair to say that the bait was going in all over the lake in small amounts. The fish couldn't go anywhere without coming across some of our bait. Fortunately the very nice Mr Richworth, Bob Baker, was making the bait by the sack load for us, and it had almost become like a natural food to the carp. At that time the LT94 was a bit scarce on the ground as if you didn't buy it by the ton, they wouldn't deal with you. So we already had a serious edge over others that fished Larkfield and other waters, namely Barden Park, Sutton and Alders. By now things had started to go wrong at Larkfield. The current leasee, LSA, had started to show signs of losing interest in the fishery. To be perfectly honest this was soul destroying as almost everyone had worked their socks off in order to maintain Larkfield as a fishery. The twelve bailliffs and the anglers had taken approximately six long, hard years to turn it from a dive into an accessible fishery with awesome looking fish in it. Perfect looking swims, all of which the bailiffs and anglers had contributed their time and effort into, and ran with the proverbial rod of iron. As head bailiff, if anyone was found pulling serious strokes, they were gone. I would take their tickets and say, "If you want it back, ask Ian Welch for it." I recently took a walk round the place and it broke my heart, the current lessee has let it slip into chronic decline. To cut a long story short it's a f****** disgrace! Human waste in loads of the swims, some of the best areas that used to produce fish are gone, and swims are completely non-existent and overgrown. The complex has been used as a source of income without putting anything back into it. No long-term stocking policy, no regeneration, nothing and ironically I recently came across by accident a forum of Kent carpers. As I read through some of the comments, like: "I was looking for somewhere to fish so recently took a walk round the old Johnson's complex, now called the Leybourne complex and it was a mess. Swims were overgrown, rubbish everywhere, crap in the swims. It looked like it had been totally neglected for years. I won't be buying a ticket for there any time soon." Plus further comments. Well congratulations go out to the current lessee - you managed to take a complex with history in Kent carp fishing going back to the sixties and you f***** it up completely. I hope you are proud of yourselves.

Tappy and I decided to go and have a look elsewhere and settled on the Johnson Snag Lake. It was a lake that had become dry during excavation work and the water table had dropped so it was left dry for approximately a year. In this time trees had shot up everywhere, saplings had taken hold but there were two large pools that held all the fish. Basically once the water levels had returned it became an underwater forest full of huge carp and tench. I know that Fred Wilton had fished it with his son-in-law Ray and done well. Then Steve Edwards and George Mills had done well, but it had been left alone for quite a while. Obviously some people were fishing it, but how seriously remained unknown. So Tappy and I decided that we would put in a serious campaign. I had been messing around with a type of natural product that includes some twenty different vegetable products, all of which are natural, but totally different to what carp were used to. We were

They loved to roam those bars!

Now thats what you call snag fishing.

Drained to build houses. GUTTED!

Steve Edwards and George Mills built the platforms

still using the LT94 base mix as we had done for the past few years, which of course was being produced under the Richworth banner. If it ain't broke, don't fix it. Anyway, back in those good old days when we still had a closed season, Tappy and I decided to start prebaiting once a week from the start of April. The plan was to put in two x 4kilo bags of bait once a week to start with for four weeks, then up it to four x 4kilo bags each twice a week.By now the weather had improved drastically and we would walk round the lake baiting up with a scoop each and just hoof it in. I remember walking up the long bank together throwing in the bait and when we got to the end we decided to walk back and see if anything was on the first lot we had put in. The sight that greeted us was incredible, the area we had put the bait in, no more than ten minuets earlier, was a heaving, bubbling cauldron of swirls, vortices and carp tails. The lake was only shallow, about four to five feet on average, with the odd deeper gulley, although about three feet where we baited. We stared at the mass of clouded, bubble infested water in front of us, then looked at each other and said, "We are gonna f****** empty the gaff!" We just couldn't wait for the start of the season.

Along came 15th June, we set up the gear and casually whiled away the hours until the mid afternoon when we were sitting back and waiting. I will never forget the circumstances . . . from somewhere was the sound of a kind of hissing. It was a hot clammy cloudy June day, but this weird sound was building momentum. We kept looking round and up to the heavens and across to the horizon, but nothing, not a hint of anything. Then as by magic we could hear a roar intensifying by the second, and far off in the distance a solid wall of water was hurtling towards us. I had never seen anything like it before or since. As the wall approached us we shouted in unison . . . "umbrellaaaaaaaaaaaaaaaaaaaaaaaaaaaaaaa." We only just got the brollies up in time as the wall of water hit us like a frigging tsunami. Jesus, the roar was incredible. We just pulled the umbrellas down over us, protecting as much tackle as we could, and as fast as the wall of water had arrived so it passed and all returned to normal. I don't think it lasted more than about five or six minutes at the most but every thing was drenched. Despite this the fishing was incredible the first night and I think I had something like seven or eight fish. Tony had about four or five. I was getting takes as I fired out pouchload after pouchload of bait. Something we had never witnessed before on Johnson's. The bait was landing over their heads in three feet of water, they never spooked, but just kept on eating. We had, however, devised a way to fish for them, because we were fishing an underwater forest. You couldn't take any chances so we used braid right through, with very soft rods. Mine were Bruce Ashby built 1lb 10oz

Harrisons with big hooks, size 2 Owners, 22lb Amnesia hooklinks, and double 18mm hookbaits. All locked up tight, no clutch, nothing. We fished with the rods no more than twelve inches away from the bedchairs at all times. If it moved, hit it . . . and do you know what we only ever lost no more than a couple of fish each. That was due to the hooklinks being cut off. The thing is, the minute you pulled into the fish the soft rod would fold over and compress then the fish would just wallow on the surface and couldn't go anywhere. You just carefully wound the fish back and into the waiting net. Admittedly the fish were a bit lively when in the net but after a few minutes they calmed down and were fine. On top of all that no fish's mouth were damaged. It always makes me chuckle when I think of how some of the clowns who fished Sutton that accused Ken Rowley of snag fishing because he was using freelined floater cake in a bed of lilies no more than twelve feet wide. It's all about how you go about your fishing. We used to watch the odd angler on the Snag Lake cast out and set their camp up some twenty feet away from their rods and then wonder why they never landed a single fish. As soon as they got a take the fish would be off, packed its bags and gone on holiday long before those blokes had even got out of their camps. It is just lamentable!

To cut a long story short, we had over one hundred carp between us in just twelve week's fishing on Johnson's Snag Lake and that's in twelve Saturday nights, not twelve week's solid fishing. We fished it that winter and still continued to catch as the temperature plummeted. There were a few very big fish in there at that time: a big long scaley fish which resembled Scaley in Larkfield, a very big common, and one in particular that I knew very well, a big deep mirror that had very wrinkly skin. I had seen that particular fish as close as two feet away on numerous occasions, and knew every single line on its body. Steve Edwards had nicknamed it the Saddle Back years previously. It would go about 40lb at the right time of year. I even lost it one winter not more than two feet from the drawstring of my landing net. It was a freezing February night, three o'clock in the morning, frost everywhere, and that beast was right in front of me in the head torch and not two feet from the drawstring. It then cut under the front of the net and rolled not more than four feet out then hit the bottom and cut my Amnesia hooklink in half on a submerged bit of metal . . . oh yes that upset me. Not as much as when we learned that the lake was due for backfilling to make way for a housing project. We were absolutely gutted to know that we wouldn't be seeing those fish again. I have to be careful what I say here, so let's just say this. The fish had alledgedly been moved from the Snag Lake after draining and put back into the Road and Island Lake but I saw a picture of a big deep bodied wrinkly looking old warrior of a carp in the pages of *Carp Talk* that weighed in at 38lb and a few ounces. Do you know what, it looked just like the Saddle Back fish from Johnson's Snag Lake. Amazing how some carp look so similar, eh? And guess what? It sure as hell didn't come out of the Road and Island Lake. There is a rumour however that before the lake was sealed off by giant hoardings and the pumping process had started a group of anglers managed to catch a large number of carp and walk the thirty yards across a bit of land that seperated the Snag Lake from the Road and Island Lake and place them out of harm's way from grubby little hands. But hey you know what rumours are like? Probably no substance to the rumours . . . eh?

Only give them a few inches . . .

I had eight fish in a night from that tree . . .

Butterscale they dont come better than that!

Split Pecs an old Larkfield warrior

That fish went crazy!

Ronan with the railway leather . . . RIP old girl

Chapter Eleven

Winter Fishing

I have been fishing winters for as long as I can remember, possibly as far back as 1970. When we first fished the Johnson's complex it was for pike. It soon became blatantly obvious that the carp were active as well. I remember someone catching a 28lb mirror from Monster Bay one January morning back in around about 1971/2. We had already seen carp moving under the ice way back in 1968/9 when guesting down at Tate & Lyle's on the second lake down from the bottom pond at Keston. The lake isn't there any more as the dam wall collapsed and is now a stream and marsh land area. We used to walk carefully on the ice in the winter; the water was only two foot six inches deep so not a problem. I wouldn't recommend anyone walking on ice at any time as it's a recipe for disaster and tragedy. Back then we would watch the wildies moving around under the ice, and if they move around, they can be caught. Winter fishing is not everyone's idea of fun, but the main reason I try and fish is because with a bit of common sense they can be caught. Plus all the fair weather hordes of anglers are gone from the lake, and you can usually catch a few without anyone knowing what you are up to. I know there is a trend in thinking that if you fill a lake in with bait during the winter, you will keep the carp looking for food. Well I can tell you that in forty years of winter fishing I can only remember that approach working three times. Once on the Johnson's Snag Lake when Tappy and I were catching them right through the winter, and on the Darenth complex and on Alders where it was said that they couldn't be caught during the winter. In fact people said that the carp shut down after about the end of November to mid December. I managed to persuade a group of lads that it was worth the effort; I could put a bait together that they would indeed eat as long as they continued to put the bait in on a discreet, regular basis. I won't deny that a bit of skulduggery took place. Only in that one of the lads had a bait boat with a fish finder on it and they used the boat to locate groups of fish then just drop a bit of bait on them. The carp were in pockets, some groups of, say, five fish and as many as ten in others but well spread out over quite an area. Now I have to say that no one sent their hook baits out on the boat, that's not cricket really, is it? But there is no harm locating and feeding the fish in that manner, is there? As far as I am aware the lads cast to the baited areas.

If there is one big edge in the winter, it's location and if no one else is fishing, then to get a small amount of bait on fish is in my opinion a massive plus. So it proved. A water that was said to be virtually impossible to catch from in the winter soon started to produce some cracking fish, in the proper winter months,

Beggar's Hole, January 1970s

from December to March. The small group of lads on the bait did very well, and they only fished weekends. The most important thing in my book for winter fishing is digestion. During the winter I want fish eating the bait, and passing it through their system as fast as can be possible, and it is possible with the right ingredients. I had already proved that on the Darenth complex many years before both on the Tip Lake and the Big Lake. The Mental Squad was catching very impressive amounts on the same bait.

I also put bait together for my old mate Ken Rowley that was based on a particular calcium caseinate that looked like casein, combined with wheat germ, blended nut meals and vitamealo plus a few additives. He really had it off all on his own whilst fishing only from about 8.30am to 4.30pm. I remember Zenon Bojko was on there at the time trying to establish Mainline Baits, and was getting very frustrated.

The biggest issue nowadays is that the amount of bait that goes in is ridiculous.

God knows who is writing articles for the magazines now but from what I have seen, I have my doubts as to how knowledgeable these people really are. On one water near us Tappy and I were catching fish right through the evil months, and in minus twelve degrees on occasions. One morning I had an ice flow in front of me, I kid you not it was at least one hundred yards long and in places up to forty-five yards wide. A north easterly had got up and the ice flow was moving towards me. I got my landing net handle and managed to ease the end of it slightly out towards my right, the wind picked it up and the whole thing swung round and drifted out across the lake and smashed into the far bank. I looked at Tappy and said, "We've got to be insane mate to be out in this." About thirty minutes later my indicator pulled up and I was into another lump. Two days later and we were back in the pouring rain and sleet. Tappy was fishing directly into the inflow where water was churning up the lake bed and discolouring over the whole area but within an hour had pulled into another thirty. It would be fair to say we were having it off. That's what is possible if you fish with a degree of common sense. Sadly a group of blokes started to turn up and fill the place in with kilo upon kilo of bait after dark. We used to sit opposite in the dark listening to them pile it in

They are out there, somewhere

As the sun set so the lake was frozen

and then during the day we would watch the bird life dive continuously hour after hour picking up their bait. That was our cue to move on to pastures new where hopefully the anglers had a bit more common sense.

It is the same with spring these days, you get to March and sometimes you get a lot of high pressure at that time of year with sunny days and very cold nights. The problem is that the majority of anglers think that's it, the weather is changing so let's pile in the bait to get the jump on everyone else baiting to gain an advantage. The trouble is it's not an advantage, just because you get a bit of sun during the day, it's still freezing at night and on a water that has an average depth of, say, fifteen feet it's going to take months to warm up - not a couple of days of sunshine. What these people don't seem to realise is that any warmth that hits the upper layers at that time of year will definitely be gone after dark when the temperature plummets.

Filling the place in with bait in the summer is not always the answer, let alone the depths of winter. I am sure some of you reading this may say, "Blimey he is one to talk; he has done his share of putting the bait in during the past," and yes I have, but, and it's a big but. For almost twenty years I haven't. The last time was when a group of us fished Larkfield and back then we were only putting between two and four kilos of bait in a session. The tench could eat that amount in no time. Plus, back then, hardly anyone was doing it. Now every Tom, Dick and Harry is at it. I've watched people pile in ten kilos in one go in March and do you know what - it doesn't work. Well not where I fish it doesn't. It makes me wonder if these blokes pile it in to try and get an edge with loads of bait because the bait is not all that good. You really don't need to pile in bait any more, carp will swim around all day long and find bait, and they can get it whenever they want in almost every swim.

On pressured waters if you take the time to look at what goes on, you will find that fish will drift into a swim where there is an abundance of bait, they may dip down and eat a couple then swim off into the next swim and eat another couple, so on and so forth. It's their world, they have the option. And that is in the warmer months, come winter you've got no chance. All the people I know who regularly catch during the winter do so because of bait choice and good angling. Not piling in bait. The only exception being on places like Pollards where you have a lot of carp but you also have huge numbers of bream and very large bream at that. Huge shoals of bream that make your toes curl up. I've known mates of mine get through forty kilos of hemp over a four day period between two or three of them. You need that amount just to keep the bream at bay. And

Atmospheric winter times

that is in December and January, frightening stuff. On most waters, where other species are quite low, I very much doubt if that approach would work. It's all relative to where you are fishing. When Tappy and I fished Johnson's Snag Lake and continued through the winter we kept catching because we kept putting in a kilo each, spread over the area we were fishing, but there wasn't a soul on there in the winter. My old mate Ted Bryan was catching consistently on Johnson's Island Lake in the winter because he just put in enough to keep the fish ticking over - just enough to feed them and keep them in the area. That is good angling not irresponsible baiting.

Another mate of mine, Duke, had fantastic results in the winter, he had worked an area whereby he was baiting a margin spot by a tree which overhung the water. Only a small tree and he was placing his baits in eight feet of water three feet from the bank. All of his takes came after dark, but the trick was to continuously top up the area. Once fish know that food is there on a regular basis but just enough to keep them wanting more it's results all the way. I lost count of the times I was indoors and a text would come through . . . "Had another one," . . . an hour later

Winter carp house at Darenth

. . . "had another one," and many a night it would be up to six fish. The fact remains that good angling in the winter catches you carp, not unlimited bait.

A lot of things have been mentioned about what attractors are best in winter and that is a tough one. I've caught on no end of things in the winter, - if you are going to use particles, then one of my favourite things would be to dye sweetcorn scarlet red and flavour it with a fruit flavour, cranberry, blackcurrant, lemon, raspberry, something like that. It's not that important. You just buy a kilo bag of frozen corn from a supermarket, throw it in a saucepan with a bottle of scarlet red dye and a heaped dessertspoonful of demerara sugar, add a dessertspoonful of flavour, bring to the boil, let it simmer for five minutes then throw it in a bucket overnight. Afterwards bag it up in small bags and you should get about six decent bags out of them. Job done. Whatever you do, don't leave it longer than over night in the bucket or the dye will reverse the process and the yellow of the corn will come back. I have no idea why but it does. I first noticed how much carp loved scarlet coloured corn about twenty-two years ago when I fished Cotton Farm for the first time. It was about January with very warm, still days and freezing, frosty nights. During the day the fish were getting right up in the shallows in about two feet of water. I had placed about twenty-five bird food baits in the shallow water and carp were all over them but not touching a single bait, which was a bit odd as I had been catching on that bait all year. Anyway I pulled out the scarlet corn and fired it out all over the area in front of me with a match angler's catapult. Within fifteen minutes the water in front of me was completely clouded up. The carp were going potty, I could have fished for them but I was more interested in their reaction. When the water cleared there wasn't a single grain of corn left out there but all the boilies I had thrown in remained. That is all I need to see, and I have used it periodically ever since when I felt the need.The last time was two winters ago and I caught well in January/February. It just works, why complicate things? I am sure there are plenty of you out there that will say that's old hat, dyed corn? Well it's only old hat if every one is doing it! If your little round balls of bait are not doing it for you, give it a go, you may even catch one or two on it. You could be lazy and buy a tin of flavoured corn from the tackle shop but where's the fun in that? Plus its not exclusive to you is it? I find it works best when every one is piling in hemp. For starters the carp are preoccupied on very small items of food so a single bit of red corn with a few bits scattered around will definitely get you a bite. You would be surprised at how many people wouldn't use that approach these days. Better for those that do then?

I am often asked what kind of flavours I think work best in winter . . . well certainly any kind of ester based flavour is good in winter. I used to buy neat esters from a mate of Nick Buss and mix them with things like geranium oil - that's the neat geranium oil not the watered down rubbish that is on sale. I had some synthetic strawberry oil made up on an ester base and that stuff emptied waters in the winter by soaking pop-ups in the neat gear. At first I had my reservations about using that stuff in such a neat format but I know a handful of guys who were fishing waters in Surrey that wouldn't use anything else in the winter because they caught so many big fish on that stuff. All those type of things . . . Martin Locke's Esterblend, Richworth's Tutti Frutti, in fact any of the acidic types will do you. Lemon is one of the all time great labels but so many people overlook it. I remember Tim Paisley writing in his column that he thought lemon was useless as a label. But here in Kent it accounted for God knows how many carp over a number of years on the quiet. I suppose it's all down to where you buy it from and what base it's on. I know it took us a very long time to find the right one to use. But you don't get much more acidic than lemon. If you look at what still works after almost forty years of being fished constantly. They come in and out of fashion all the time. Pineapple, tutti, maple, cream, condensed milk etc. There is a reason for it. Carp are attracted to them as labels, it's that simple. Provided the base ingredients don't change, then they will continue to work.

Like I've said before on many occasions, there are far more carp anglers caught on advertising than actual carp! If something comes out in a blaze of publicity, then stay well clear, unless you see someone you know actually using it and catching on it. What happened to Ambio or whatever it was called? This is it! The world would take notice of this gear, it's going to empty every lake in the country. So where is it now then? Probably down the plug hole with all the other overrated rubbish. I guess the most consistent, successful method on pressured waters will be the most inventive. If all you do is fire out the same old round boilies just like everyone else, then it's a lottery, isn't it because you are doing exactly the same as anyone else.

Maggots are good at any time of year but there are maggots and there are maggots. Rob Maylin had fantastic results during the winter a few years ago using big PVA bags full of them with his magaligner rig. So did Martin Locke by using gallons of them, but once that approach has been flogged to death it becomes like every thing else, average. Soups are very good in the winter. If you have been getting good results on your chosen bait on your lake through the year, then just grind up a kilo of the bait. Add it to the lake water slowly until you have a thick type of soup and just spod it out in a large spod that creats a cloud of your going bait into the area you are fishing. The shallower the depth the better. You will only need a couple of spods into the area, and just fish a square bait over the top to make it different. That has worked incredibly well for me during the spring, especially when all others are piling in the bait. If you want to catch fish consistently these days, then you need to be different. Consider this, if you sit and watch all those wonderful DVDs that show you how carp react in underwater situations or that tell you how to go out and catch loads of carp in the winter, then you can bet your bottom dollar that there are loads of others who have done what you have done. They can't be bothered to do something different for themselves, that is hardly what you call pioneering fishing is it? You are just like the other sheep. OK, fair enough if you haven't been fishing for long, I suppose those DVDs may give you an idea, or a starting point, but if you have any idea of what you are doing, then avoid them like the plague. They will lead you down the proverbial garden path. Do it for yourself, an idea born of your own hard work is far more rewarding than copying someone else. Not only that but if you discover a method that works for you, then you are the only one who knows about it, unlike all the people watching a DVD that's open to the general public. It's not rocket science is it?

Base mixes can play a huge part in your results; bird food mixes can be very good in the winter, providing you use the better types. There are a lot of ready made bird food type baits out there that I wouldn't touch with a barge pole, you only have to look at some of them to realise that there is not a lot of actual bird food in there. If there was, they would not roll in commercial bait rolling machines. You need at least fifty percent bird food in a bait in the winter, and the only people who can get that to roll successfully are those who roll their own baits on rolling tables, not in commercial machines. I personally have had far more success on the coarser types of rearing food; I have used the same rearing food now for around twenty-five years or more, which comes from Holland. It is along the lines of seed but not as expensive and I buy it in twenty kilo sacks. As far as I am aware no bait companies use it and whenever I have asked the supplier if anyone else orders it, he always says, no, only the rearers of canaries. Ironically it's the most consistent ingredient within a bait I have ever used and unlike fishmeals and meat meals/meat proteins it is the most adaptable base mix that will lend itself to a wide range of applications at that time of year. Ask anyone who has used my old bird food mix Factor 7 since I formulated it all those years ago and they will probably say it has accounted for God knows how many successful baiting campaigns. I remember when the Darenth Tip Lake was being dominated by fishmeal baits that we were told there was no chance that a crap bird food bait would work on there in the winter. Three months later it was said that if you were not on Haswell's Factor 7 mix, you couldn't get a bite! How fickle are carp anglers, eh?

The fact remains with bait that sometimes just being different with bait is all that is required. Yes there is a case for food value baits. I have great faith in them at the right time, but just because some waters are very rich and abundant in natural food deposits doesn't mean that high value food bait is a guaranteed winner over a bait that on the surface is deemed inferior. Quite often it can be the reverse! I honestly hand on heart believe that these days in most cases it is down to what is being used most on a particular water. I think Rob Maylin hit the nail on the head when he said that unless the bloke fishing next to him was catching three times more than he was on expensive baits, then that is not a road he would go down. Or words to that effect. You only have to look at what Rob has caught on his cheaper baits to realise that a bait carp will readily accept as food coupled with good angling ability takes a lot of beating. Look at the success of Mike Willmott's Shellfish B5. Is it a high value food bait? I have no idea, but if it contains the magic brown powder I know Mike gets hold of, then it is little wonder it is so successful. Having used it myself, I can verify that the addition of that product definitely turns a good bait into an outstanding one, no question about it. I don't really take much notice of what I see on the internet concerning bait and the self-appointed bait experts that you see on there. At the end of the day you normally find that there is a financial commitment required when you get to the end of the expert's sermon . . . well there's a change? There can be no doubt that bait is confidence, get your bait right and then you can concentrate on angling for your particular quest.

Another word of warning would be that just because some bloke can quote all the chemical or scientific terms or a formula for each and every protein chain, it doesn't make him an expert. And there have been a few of them out there over the years. I even read from one piece that apparently carp spook when confronted by the same chemical flavour base that has been used too much on a particular water." . . . really? I must give Bob Baker a ring and let him know so that he can remove Tutti-Frutti and Pineapple Hawian from his range of flavours as obviously they are no good any more! Look at the bloke putting carp on the bank - he is the one you need to be talking to. As long as I've known Fred Wilton, and that's a very long time, on the few occasions I've had the privilege to talk about bait with him, or listen to what he has had to say, or even in correspondence, not once have I heard him ramble on giving scientific terms or equations. In fact quite the opposite and all explained in layman's terms in an understandable fashion, unless of course he just thinks I'm stupid. That is always a possibility. I have correspondence from Fred where he was explaining why a particular herring meal was so much more beneficial and digestible, plus carp could utilise far more of the base product than acid casein. Not once did he need to ramble on about scientific factors. Robin Red, along with its compatible complimentary ingredient, is a fantastic winter bait that I, along with others, have used it to great effect in the winter. I remember a certain so-called bait expert explaining just how you should only use about ten percent of Robin Red in a bait. Well if that is correct, then Ian Booker's Robin Red bait really shouldn't have worked at all then? But it did, in fact that bait emptied lake after lake in terms of fish captures, especially in the winter. Ha, ten percent, I personally wouldn't throw that out on the lawn for the birds! Maybe that so-called bait expert was feeling somewhat embarrassed by the fact that he had stuck his nose in where it wasn't wanted in a company that supplies bird feeds and particles to anglers and now charges more to anglers than it does to bird enthusiasts. Also resulting in the price of Robin Red going up from what was sixty quid a twenty-five kilo sack to now about £140 a twenty-five kilo sack. Hmm, yes I think I would be embarrassed too as now no one can afford to put in the right amount of Robin Red in a bait as it's too f****** dear! It's a very true saying that a little knowledge can be a dangerous thing, eh? I know I can say a few abrasive words here and there, but really carp anglers should keep well away from trying to interfere with things that result in other carp anglers paying more for in the long run. There are very few edges around in carp fishing these days so to protect those edges, in my opinion is very important. Those of you that stick it out each winter in order to catch a few decent fish and to get out there when the lakes are much, much quieter will know exactly what I mean. Winter fishing is hard work, with long cold nights and quite often you will be sitting there in evil, cold north easterly winds, or freezing rain or sleet.

Winter fishing is an acquired taste, but on that odd occasion when that indicator moves up and you pull into a lump then it has all been worth the trouble, hasn't it? We are all different, and have different goals, me personally I prefer to fish a water that will give me a return for my efforts. On some occasions I have caught as many as six fish in a night during the winter. By winter I mean December to March and all of them after dark. Some waters can come alive after dark, and others will only produce during the day. Plus it can be somewhat surprising just where carp can be caught from in the winter. By that I mean in what depth of water. I have caught fish in as little as three feet of water and as deep as twenty-seven feet. The hardest thing is to determine what is going on in your chosen venue as it's all down to effort. One water Tappy and I fished during the winter only came alive after dark. Then it was like another lake. Within an hour or so of most people going home the fish would start to show and loads of them. We would sit there sometimes watching in disbelief at the amount of activity that would go on. You would get lots of liners, then takes…it was mental. The hardest thing is to keep it quiet if you are catching fish regularly. Someone finds out and the last thing you want is for a group of anglers to turn up and fill in the lake with bait because they think that they will have the advantage. As that is in my opinion not how it works at all. I know all this sounds a bit devious but I see no harm whatsoever in protecting your fishing. And if that means not telling another angler the whole truth then so be it. I would never mislead another angler on purpose - that is out of order as I have had it done to me and it is not very nice. Fortunately the older you get, the wiser you get and with that you get to know who you can trust. Whose word you can take as gospel and those who should never be listened to under any circumstances. As slippery as it sounds if you are catching fish during the winter, then I would keep it very close to my chest. Most of the decent blokes will shake your hand and say well done if they know you are catching through all your hard work. Then there are the ones who will just jump in on what you are doing and ruin it for everyone. Because that's how carp fishing can be at times these days. Fishing etiquette among carp anglers is not what it was. I don't mean to sound negative but certainly where I have been fishing over the last few years it is the case. Winter fishing is all about effort, and effort reaps rewards. It is all about picking the right water for you and what you want out of your fishing. Some will target big fish and others will just be happy to get a few takes. Personally I prefer a few takes with the odd chance of a decent fish thrown in. I want to enjoy my fishing - it can be bloody freezing in winter, why make it hard for yourself? If I am sitting out in the cold, then I want to see those indicators pulling up to the butt, and feel the satisfying tug on the end of the rod as another fish plods off . . .

A nice scaley winter mirror

The business end of things

Gary and Rodney in December with a field testing brace on the Factor 7

Darenth carp, ugly? Never!

Young Wes had his share on the Factor 7

A winter brace for Rocky

Ken got it right in the winter on a protein/nut mix with condensed milk

A big bait eating monster

Chapter Twelve

A Look at Baits

I have had an avid interest in bait and all its simplicities and complexities for what has seemed like forever. The reality is that from about the time Ken Rowley, Steve Edwards and I started using maggots for carp fishing I had an inner desire to know just why something was working. I remember when Steve, Ken and I were guesting the lower pond in the grounds of Tate & Lyle at Keston to fish for the wildies. We used to use stale Hovis crust for floating bait but Steve went one better when he cut an orange in half and squeezed the juice onto his Hovis hookbait. It seemed the carp could find it quicker. I had to know why, just as I had to know why it was that maggots that were bred and fed on fish offal were without doubt larger and more appealing to the carp than those bred and fed on meat offal. Some may not care why. But that attitude never got you anywhere in terms of learning about what does or doesn't get you results. It was around 1967 that Ken managed to source a supply of maggots in bulk. At the time Ken had a deal to start to produce his own carp rods called the Rowley Carp Rod and was working on the design and blanks through Ken Brown's Fishing Tackle shop in Holmesdale Road, Bromley. It was the only decent shop around at the time that had specialist carp tackle in stock: Richard Walker hooks, Goldstrike hooks (were what we used back then) and low water salmon hooks, on which we cut down the ends and put on solder blob. It was there that Ken Brown revealed the whereabouts of his supplier of maggots to Ken. It was a Polish geezer who had a maggot farm over in Parsonage Lane, North Cray. I remember going over there with Ken and you could smell the farm from about a quarter of a mile away. Jesus, the place stank . . . as soon as you got to the bloke's entrance the smell of ammonia took your breath away. We used to buy a huge square tin full up with maggots for five quid. We called it a gallon but it was probably a darn sight more than that - more like two gallons. He used to save us the uncleaned maggots from the bottom of the vat that held them. Down there would be fish tails, bones and all manner of bits and pieces in the tin. Ken's motor used to stink for days after. Now you could ask what has all this to do with bait. Well it's got everything to do with it! I personally think that it was the fact that the maggots bred on fish that made them far superior to anything else we had come across. They were probably twice the size of normal meat bred maggots, and of course who is to say that those maggots were not impregnated with the smell of fish meal? And we all now know just how much carp like the fishmeals, don't we. Or was it the smell of ammonia that attracted the carp? We will never know because the bait farm was closed down because of the complaints of the localish residents who protested about the smell. That in itself is not important, what is, however, is that for whatever reason the carp found those maggots more attractive than any other type of maggots. There can be no doubt about the fact that those Keston carp, some would say notoriously difficult to catch, were far more attracted to those maggots than anything else at that time. Ken, Steve and I were getting crazy results using them at times. I have mentioned in another publication that I had four takes in a night's fishing at Keston, that alone was more than a lot of others had in a year's fishing on there, let alone one night. It certainly wasn't because I was a better angler but because we had an edge, and a huge one. In my opinion that is always going to be paramount in helping you achieve results.

In about 1971/2 Steve Edwards had managed to get Fred Wilton to allow us to use his PYM (Phillips Yeast Mixture) bait. Steve had already used Fred's baits and I think he had met Fred in the mid 60s. By Fred's own admission he was the second person to use the protein bait. I remember Ken and I meeting up with Steve on the dam wall at Keston when Steve had just come hotfoot from Fred's with a huge cardboard box in his hands. We waited in anticipation and excitement as Steve opened the box and as he did so a fine brown powder erupted into the air and our nostrils were filled with an incredibly rich, savoury aroma, the likes of which we had not known before. It is well documented about the PYM so I won't go into the whys and wherefores of something that is already written about. I will ask if you have any idea what it feels like to be using something that would create history? The secrecy involved, the drama, and the sheer determination of others who would do anything to find out what you were using? The underhanded tricks used to try and find out the ingredients of the bait. What you also have to remember is that we were at times catching up to ten carp a day using Fred's baits - I kid you not when I say that would quite literally be the tally of a whole season's carp for many people at that time. So it was little wonder others would try anything to find out what you had as bait. I will say that I would still to this day use PYM if it was around in its original form. What a lot of people don't know is that the type of yeast that was produced in Germany which gave PYM that rich aroma and taste profile was discontinued in the mid seventies. I had a long and interesting chat with the owner of Phillips and he told me that the factory which was producing that type of yeast was closed down and that type of yeast was never produced again as the main product that formed part of that yeast was no longer available. It is the same with many products that become unavailable as it is all about the quality of the base ingredients. If you don't have those, you don't have a thing, end of story.

It always makes me chuckle when I read about or listen to people who try and replicate something, a flavour, an ingredient, or an oil. Whatever, it will never be the same. Loads of people try these days to replicate a flavour but the truth is you can't. I know from personal experience as there were two flavours that I used to mix together with an amino compound. It wasn't my idea but someone else's, who passed it on to me. That combination absolutely emptied everywhere it was used in the summer, autumn and winter. It didn't matter where it was used either, it caught everywhere and in any conditions. As a label for a bait it was, in my opinion, second to none. The fact was that the flavour company that produced it could no longer produce it because the base ingredients that formed the natural side of it were no longer available. I was absolutely gutted. This was twenty-six years ago and trust me I have tried through God knows how many sources ever since to get something remotely close to it made. The fact of the matter is you can't . . . none of the copies I have received were even close. I also had a synthetic strawberry oil blended with esters to produce an incredible label for birdfood baits, and those who used it, especially during autumn and winter, were stacking them up. I called it Esterberry.

Several of my friends used to just glug pop-ups in it for three to four months prior to winter and just catch and catch using single baits. Again, anywhere, it didn't matter. Once more that became unavailable. As it was mainly synthetic I tried to get what little I had left copied by one of the country's best flavour houses, not a chance although it smelt the same and I used it religously but to no avail. Once again proving to me personally that you just can't reproduce something without the base ingredients.

Going back to the grief caused over bait, it could be argued that the reason all the bait companies exist is due to Fred's publication of *Towards the Ultimate Bait* that was reproduced in *The Carp*. Fred had, let's say, allowed a couple of guys to use one of his baits, two very well known anglers too, and they were going to write an article claiming they had invented an HNV bait . . . naughty, naughty. So Fred published his theory to stop them getting any credit for all of his hard work. Of course that led to the bait explosion of protein, HNV etc. That's why I always smile when I see or read something from a so-called bait expert claiming this, that and the other. If it wasn't for Fred, they wouldn't have a clue, it was all his years of pioneering work and the publication of that article that set up all these people. I don't think that Fred ever really got the credit he deserved for the bait revolution. He was light years ahead of anyone else at that time, and arguably still is if the results of his, and his friends', barbel captures are anything to go by. No wonder he distanced himself from carp fishing.

Moving on to less provocative topics, I am going to skip the subject of milk proteins other than to use them as reference. Why? Because I wouldn't pretend to know enough about them to write in an authorative fashion, nor do I think they are any longer relative to my thinking on bait. That doesn't mean I don't think there is a place for them nowadays, just not in my style of fishing. The world of bait can be a very seedy place and I would like to give you some true examples of just how seedy it has been. During my time using milk proteins I came across some outrageous examples of why I hardly trust anyone, that was then and it still goes on today. I had been struggling to obtain a decent source of casein, but Fred very generously gave me the name of a company in Acton who were producing an acid casein that was precipitated on hydrochloric acid. They also produced the best calcium caseinate I have ever used, not the light and fluffy stuff, but a type more in common with casein. That stuff really turned them on their heads, especially in winter. Eventually that casein became known as Dutch Acid Casein. Probably the best casein ever produced in terms of what percentage the carp could easily digest compared to the New Zealand and French caseins. I think I had used that particular casein for about six years and it was starting to become very hard to obtain as good old Europe was as usual flexing its muscles and restricting the inportation of it to the UK. I think we had that casein to ourselves for a good few years before word started to get out. As the supplies started to dwindle, like an idiot I got carried away and panicked in case I couldn't get any more and phoned up a major bait company in Essex which was claiming they had a source of the said casein. I should have known better as once before I had purchased a casein from a so-called reputable bait company and it turned out to be the kind of casein that is used for making TV screens. I wasted three months of my time on a hard water using that garbage. I should have smelt a rat when the geezer offered me a huge sack of this supposed Dutch Acid Casein that, if my memory serves me well, we never bought that casein in any larger size sacks than twenty kilos. I took his word for it as he said the company he had bought it from bagged it up in larger size sacks for him. I paid him 240 quid for that sack as it would have lasted me all year. When I got it home I did the poor man's water test on it, (basically if you want to test casein and its dipersability or digestability, you just take a cup of boiling water and put in a teaspoonful of the casein and stir it) if the casein seperates into granules, it's a decent drop of gear, but if it hangs off the spoon like a load of old snot, it's rubbish. This lot was clinging to the spoon like a bat hanging from a cave roof . . . I went mental. I was straight on the phone to the geezer and threatened him, I told him the very next article I wrote I would expose him as a f****** con artist! Needless to say he said to come straight over and pick up the cash and he even gave me petrol money for my inconvenience. While I was there he begged me not to blow the whistle on him, which I didn't, but anyone who asked me what I thought of his bait company I would say I wouldn't touch the geezer with a barge pole. I dread to think how many unsuspecting anglers that clown sold duff gear to. I remember a major bait company was having all sorts of problems with caseins and all their bait was floating. Lee Jackson asked me if I could suggest a supply of casein for this bait company, as he was friendly with them. I was happy to do as I quite liked the guys who ran the company. I do believe they were buying their casein from a company in Beckenham, Kent and as it wasn't far from me I arranged to go over and take a look at their products. To cut a long story short, it was awful. I did a few tests on the caseins etc, and it was rubbish. No wonder their baits were floating. I mention this because the biggest single factor in bait formulation is the ingredients. If you don't have fresh, reliable ingredients, then you don't have a bait in the first place. Just one single duff ounce of anything in your bait and you may as well cast up a tree and leave it there. That's why I look at some of the so-called bait experts' recipes and think to myself, Jesus there must be fifteen different ingredients in that bait and if it goes wrong, there is no way you can tell what is wrong with it. I certainly wouldn't buy a product that didn't show at least nine months shelf life on the sack label. Simplicity is by far the most efficient way to produce reliable bait as there is less to go wrong with it and the longer that bait will last as a food source. I have stuck with some base mixes for six or seven years without changing it. I know some blokes these days who change their baits every five minuets by comparison. I've come across some blokes that have three different baits with them at times. That achieves nothing as far as I am concerned, and shows a lack of belief in your bait.

Ever since I started using Fred Wilton's baits all those years ago I had it instilled in me that you get your bait right then stick with it. Establishing bait as a consistent food source is a marathon not a sprint, you have to believe in what you are doing and in the long term you will definitely benefit. It is forty years now since I first used Fred's baits and in all that time I have only had three occasions when I wasn't confident in the bait I was using. Once when I had no input into the bait, it turned out to be rubbish and twice more when Tony Tappenden and I had some bait made up once by a bait company giant who stitched us up by not putting in what they said they were putting in it. The previous winter we emptied waters on a particular bait and then the next year the bait wasn't the same. Having spoken to someone who knew what we were using, they told us that we definitely didn't have the same bait as the year before as they knew the guy who made up the bait and he definitely left out the key ingredient. It showed in our results and was the last time we gave someone a chance to make up our bait. He clearly didn't listen to how it had to be prepared. So it is little wonder I trust hardly anyone. Those I would trust however are Tony at Premier Baits, Martin Locke's Solar products, Mike Willmott's Essential Products, John Baker, Bob Baker's Richworth Baits, and Steve at Ace Baits. All of these I have used products from or had baits made by them and I have been happy with them and caught plenty of fish on the products. I know all of those people well and trust them to supply me with products that are reliable. Yes, I am in a fortunate position whereby I know exactly what I am using from those companies or individuals, and I am also aware that if you as an angler want bait, then in general you have to trust in the company that supplies your bait or make it yourself. That is a long process in the learning curve. What does scare me, however, is that I have been approached by at least three people over the years who are running their own bait companies or starting out, and they have asked me to give them addresses of suppliers for ingredients, oils, flavours, additives, enhancers. You must be joking, yeah I am going to hand over all those years of hard work, success, failure, tracking down products and sourcing all sorts of stuff, just like that. Because so and so wants to start a bait company and wants me to hand over knowledge that has taken me forty years to obtain . . . it ain't going to happen, is it? And they have the nerve to ask you with a straight face as well. That's the problem nowadays, a lot of people want something for nothing without actually doing any hard work for it. Well not from me they won't. If those people need to ask without actually doing some of the work themselves, then are they really the type of people you want making your bait? In my opinion it takes years and years to become knowledgeable on bait, not five minutes and a few ideas from so and so. If you are going to produce your own bait for, say, a group of you to have a campaign, then you really need to source the right products.

I don't quite know how to put this in a diplomatic way but there are a lot of companies out there selling all manner of ingredients and in my opinion some of them should be prosecuted under the trade descriptions act. I have seen companies offering things like Vitamealo. Trust me there is no such thing now. It isn't made any more and to my knowledge the last proper sack I personally bought was probably somewhere around three years ago. What you will probably be buying is Lamlac, Bounty or something like it, and most of the calf milk replacers available are nothing like Vitamealo. It was John Baker who very kindly gave me his contact for a Vitamealo supplier. The true Vitamealo would, as you open the sack, send a microscopic cloud into the air and you would immediately notice the aroma of

Vanalin, a very sweet rich creamy aroma/taste which covers you in a sticky kind of powder. If you buy a product under the name of Vitamealo and it doesn't do that, then it isn't Vitamealo. Trust me it isn't.

It is the same with LT94. As far as I am aware Steve Edwards was the first person to know about LT94 and Peter Springate was I think, the first to use it in a bait. All I did was arrange to purchase it in bulk from the main supplier by the ton through my bait company name. That was as long ago as twenty years or so now. That particular herring meal was the Rolls Royce of fishmeals at the time; it had a biological digestible protein content of ninety percent. I remember getting correspondence from Fred Wilton suggesting that it was a better source of digestible protein than casein. In my opinion you could not get a better recomendation than that although Fred felt that for his usage he prefered casein because fishmeals had that overriding smell that just couldnt be masked. Even that has changed now and will continue to do so as once again the base ingredients are getting harder to find. I have seen some samples of LT94 in the last year that I wouldn't touch with a barge pole. Tony at Premier baits has a source of LT94 which is exactly the same product that we used in the beginning - very fine powder which is consistant right through. The batches from other supplies of LT94 are nothing like this. They are inconsistent and quite clearly have other fish included in the batch. They are easy to spot as they have lots of what look like small dark blotches in the meal. It actually looks a lot like the old CLO has been mixed in with it. There can be no doubt in my mind that this kind of LT94 is nowhere near as effective as the pure herring meal. I personally would be very wary of what you buy under the banner of LT94 and there are a lot of people selling it on the internet and it is very expensive. This of course is not a gaurantee of success as quite often it is all down to what is being used and where you are fishing. There are those who will tell you that by using a superior food source it will give you a better chance of catching big fish and that is not necessarily the case.

Let us backtrack a few years to about the time I started to wonder just how effective the milk protein baits were. Something was changing, I can remember talking to Steve Edwards and saying that something was not right . . . I had been fishing a complex near Sevenoaks, and Steve had been fishing further down in Kent. The results we were getting were very similar in that if we went down to the lake and had, say five fish in a day, one of the others would go the next day and have two fish, then someone else went down the next day and blanked. For the next couple of days nothing was caught and then all of a sudden bang, four or five fish come out by those on the bait and it would then taper off again. That pattern started to repeat itself over and over again. We came to the conclusion that the fish just couldn't digest the milk protein baits as fast as we thought. It was as though they were becoming full up on the amount of bait we were putting in, just couldn't digest it quickly enough and so just stopped eating the stuf. At about this time my old friend Colin Cameron started to fish the same lake as me and was using basically a fish flavoured semolina/soya flour type bait and was stacking them up one after the other. It was now turning to winter but it was quite clear they were eating and digesting the bait he was using much more quickly. Every time he put a fish on the mat it was passing shedloads of digested bait. They were just swimming around eating and passing it all out. That was the last time I ever used milk protein baits. To this day I think it is something a little deeper than that.

I then started looking at birdfood type baits, which were just starting to be used, as maybe an alternative to milk proteins. I first put my own kind of birdfood mix together around the early eighties or thereabouts. I like to be different where I can and I had sourced a particular rearing food from Holland that, as far as I am aware, definitely wasn't being used here. Ironically the only importer of that product that I am aware of has always said that I am the only person from a bait company to buy it from him as he was, and still is, only supplying the breeders of canaries with small amounts. He has never been approached by anyone to do with fishing which, I find amazing in this day and age. Personally I wouldn't use anything other than a highly digestible bait in the winter and adding wheatgerm always adds to the effectiveness at this time. I wouldn't use it in the summer as in the wrong hands it can go off very quickly. I know there are those who still claim that fishmeals work in the winter, and that is thier prerogative but that's OK if you are the only one doing it and you have a decent, easily digestible bait. Tony Tappenden and I caught shedloads of winter carp on the LT94 mix on Johnson's, but we were the only ones doing it. Peter Springate was turning over Fork Pond on the same bait but he too was in the minority using it. All these things are relative and affect what you do and how you do it. Bait can be as easy as you want it to be or as difficult as you make it. Looking back through my bait recipe diaries I can see that I never made bait that had more than six ingredients in it. Usually fifty percent would be either a protein source or bulk ingredient; the other fifty percent would be fats, carbohydrates, vitamin, minerals and solubles. Nice and simple, making sure that everything is fresh, no dodgy ingredients that you don't know how old they are. It's a simple motto . . . no shelf life confirmation, no inclusion. What a lot of people don't realise is that you have no idea how long a product has been sitting in a warehouse. If you buy off the internet, does your sack of gear turn up with a best before sticker on it? Or a date when the product was bagged? When I was buying in bulk I always got paperwork or there would be a ticket label stating when the product was bagged or produced. Reduce that figure by three months and that is probably about right. Once you have made sure that everything is fresh then, if you can afford to, you would be better off getting large quantities rolled and frozen at the same time, it won't come to any harm then.

Never, ever leave baits in the bag that you take from the freezer without opening the bag first to let them air. Never, ever leave baits in a bag in a car in the summer; the heat within that bag will rise drastically turning your bait off in no time at all. Roy (Rocky) Ashdown made that mistake on the Johnson Railway Lake some years ago. We were all on the same bait on Larkfield, Rocky went on the Railway and was baiting up and the fish were well on the bait. He had already caught a handful of fish, but he made the mistake of leaving a few four kilo bags in his car to defrost. As it was quite windy outside he thought it was OK, but with the sun on the windows the temperature inside the car was boiling hot. He then took the baits from the car and unbeknown to him he was firing out rancid bait that cost him big time. He had to start all over again with another bait. You really don't need that on any water, let alone those kinds of waters.

Some waters can be very difficult to establish a bait on, mainly because they are very rich waters that are constantly under angling pressure. The pressure is on 24/7 with no break in the fishing. I personally think the abolishment of the closed season was a massive mistake. How many big fish have died in mysterious circumstances since they abolished it? It's the same old excuse every time . . . we don't know what the fish died of, there were no signs of disease etc. Well stress is a huge killer of humans, so who is to say that the same kind of stress on fish constantly fished for without any break in the relentless pursuit of them by anglers is not enough to kill them? This brings me to baiting circumstances. Carp are subjected to a constant barrage and bombardment of bait, be it spring, summer, winter or autumn but particularly winter and spring. Who on earth in their right mind piles in the bait at that time of year? But they do. Tappy and I were fishing Pollards Lake in the winter and we were catching good carp in minus eight degrees. A right result by anyone's standards. We did the odd night and, believe this or not, people were coming round in the early hours of the morning piling in bait! What a bunch of complete clowns . . . what sort of idiot advocates the use of that amount of bait at that time of year. During the daylight hours we used to watch the birds diving constantly and picking up bait. All that those blokes were doing was basically feeding the ducks, coots and tufties during the winter. It's exactly the same in the spring, the sun comes out and so do the clowns with their bait buckets. What is wrong with you? Has someone who wants their five minutes of fame in a monthly carp fishing magazine suggested that you need to pile in the bait once the sun comes out? Well, if you take notice of people like that, then you are just as bad! The air temperature is warm but the water is freezing. Tappy knows divers who go down regularly in the spring and even though the air temperature is warm the water temperature is eight to ten degrees in an average of fourteen feet of water. Do you really think carp will be scoffing kilo after kilo of bait in those conditions? If you do, then you shouldn't be carp fishing because all you are doing is killing your own fishing and everyone else's along with it. The only time I have personally known waters respond to a regular supply of bait in the winter is when you have a high density of carp in a lake and you are the only ones doing it. Other than that, for as long as I have known, your chances of catching carp in the winter are greatly increased when you use just hookbaits only. In case you don't know it, carp really do know what those little round things are, and at a time when carp are not moving around enough to burn off enough energy to make them feed, you really don't need to put in loads of bait. Contrary to what you read in the weeklies or monthlies, piling in bait can be the kiss of death for you and those around you. Think of it this way, if you have a bait out there on its own, then if a carp is interested then you have a very good chance of a pick up. If you put out ten baits, that is reduced to a ten to one chance of hooking a carp. If you put out a kilo of 14 mm baits, you have just reduced the odds of a take to, say, two hundred to one! That really is not good odds is it? Look, no offence, but just because Joe Bloggs writes for a carp fishing magazine, it doesn't make him right. You can always put in bait if the carp are eating it, but you just can't take it out if they are not and that is the problem.

I can honestly say that I have only messed up once in terms of a baiting campaign, and getting it completely wrong, that was on Horton, Pete Springate, Stuart Gillham, Steve Edwards and I were using a bait containing the LT94, which at the time wasn't really known about. We knew how good it was as we had caught shedloads of fish on it elsewhere, but Horton was a different prospect. We thought we could take a short cut and just fill the lake in and that would be it. Wrong (so yes, hands up, I've been guilty of it myself!) but it's if you learn from your mistakes that counts . . . we were walking round Horton with a wheelbarrow full of bait, and I mean full - thousands of baits that we just chucked in with the vain hope of success. We failed, mind you I only fished about seven nights that first year, not conducive to catching on Horton. I did manage to get one take, which I lost to a hookpull and then I only did three nights the second year. That's not an excuse but a fact. I was in the process of losing my house in the recession and didn't have my fishing head on properly but Dave Lane and his mates got it right. They were baiting sensibly where the carp were feeding, which will always be a better option than our approach of trying to do it the wrong way by piling in the bait. Strangely enough Ted Bryan and Graham Hackett and I had loads of fish out of Barden Park on that Horton bait, the application was different, and the fish not so pressured either. That was a massive lesson learned about what not to do in terms of a baiting campaign.

Another thing worth remembering is that there will always be those who say that you should always use a food bait when targeting big fish. Of course they are entitled to their opinion, but you may find that just about every big fish that has been targeted has been caught on any number of things and not just a food bait. Most of the time those who recommend the use of food baits either run the company that supplies that type of bait, or are promoting that company who recommends that type of bait. Or they are a field tester who stands to gain something from promoting that bait. For a perfect example, let's take one of today's so-called superstars, the guy fishes full time, he has an unlimited supply of bait, is probably paid a premium to fish and promote that bait or the company's products. Good luck to him, but the reality is that if that company's products are so good, then why change companies so often, and they do don't they? Some anglers probably change bait companies more often than they change their underwear! So what does that tell you? Those same anglers still catch their fair share of fish, don't they? It tells me that it is all down to the bloke behind the rod! And to a certain extent it is irrelevant at times what those blokes use.

A large percentage of catches are certainly helped immensely by the time an angler puts in on the water he is fishing. I know because I've done it myself at times. I was on Alders a few years back and I had a week where I had no work so I planned to fish from 5.00am to about 11.00am each morning which was the most productive time. I would bait up with a kilo of bait when I left the lake, and would get straight back in the swim the next morning at 5.00am, pack up at around 11 o'clock, fire out the bait, and so on. I never blanked, and it made it look like I was having it right off. Well I was because I was fishing effectively, at the right time, leaving a continuous food source for the carp. From 11.00am in the morning right through until I got there at 5.00am the next morning, there were no lines in the water as they fed on my freebies . . . it's not rocket science, is it? It was then that I learned never to envy those who look like they are catching all the time because they are not. They are there when the fish are feeding so clearly an advantage if you are at the lake all week. Bait does not necessarily give you an automatic advantage. Especially a food value bait. It definitely did years ago but I am not convinced it does any more on your average pressured water. On most of them these days there are so many different types of baits going in that lake that you can't tell me that the carp can swim around that lake and by taking a mouthful of bait from each swim that it can determine which bait has done it the most good. Not a chance!

Most of the experienced blokes I know all use their own choice of bait, no matter what it is. Over the course of a year they will all catch their fair share of carp, and the only relevant factor between their results will be how much time they have put in. I know blokes who wouldn't dream of using any of the bait company baits that are out there, and yet they still manage to catch an incredible amount of carp. On some of the waters I've fished, Sutton-at-Hone being a prime example. An angler I know, who most of you have never even heard of, won't have anything to do with publicity or magazines, but when I was on there he was top rod by a mile. He caught about six times the fish that one of the country's superstars had caught, and in about a third of the time the the superstar had put in. So all things are relevant in terms of bait and application. A lot of anglers out there also believe that new products or attractors or highly publicised products are best in terms of results, again that is a misconception. Just because some flavours or attractors are considered old hat, that doesn't make them redundant.

I once believed that flavours were just labels for a food bait but I don't any more. There are far too many instances where some particular flavours, esters, oils, amino compounds etc have consistently produced results for those who stick with them through thick and thin, regardless of what base mix they are used in. This could be a food source bait or an attractor type bait. In fact some cheap ingredient type baits consistently catch carp year in year out regardless of what others may tell you. If their words of knowledge are so true, then how come so-called cheap type baits like Richworth's Tutti Fruiti or Pineapple Hawaiian continue to account for God knows how many carp each year? I mention Richworth's because they were the first bait company to mass produce baits for carp and general anglers. Those two baits alone have accounted for an incredible amount of fish each year, and for donkey's years too. Others have simply jumped on the ready made, high attract, flavour bandwagon.Some of these acidic type flavours actually come into their own during the spring, and can have a very limited period whereby they simply outfish most other type of baits. A lot of people won't thank me for it, but for whatever reason, as far back as I can remember, Richworth Pineapple Hawaiian bottom baits or pop-ups have always come into their own during the spring, on so many waters that I fished. This was especially so on hard waters where they really produce the goods. Over the last eight years it is blatantly obvious that by the end of May you just can't buy a take on them. Obviously I am talking about the anglers whom I know use them on waters that are in my area of fishing. I wouldn't comment on anywhere else but it really is weird, maybe it's a colour thing - I don't know. The results don't lie, maybe it is an acidic thing connected to the pH of the water in the spring, who knows.

For a long time now I have believed that a carp's dietary requirements change about three times a year, pre-spawning, post-spawning, and autumn/winter. That's why I don't believe there is such a thing as an all year round individual bait. One bait just won't cover it. You can't possibly cater for the changes and dietary requirements of carp in one bait in my opinion. I know that in the tests I have carried out with friends and by myself that a slight change of ingredients at the right time of year can really lift your results, absolutely no question. To be perfectly honest I don't have the time or the inclination any more to go chasing rainbows but I firmly believe in that statement, and have seen the results to prove it. Whether you believe it or not I think there is evidence to suggest that this is a possibility. Of course the good thing is that bait companies couldn't possibly cater for a change in carp's requirements, it would be impractical and unrealistic to effectively alter commercial bait three times a year. Those of you who make their own bait and who have similar beliefs can indeed afford to try it.

There are other topics that are incredibly valid, like are there ingredients or certain flavour bases that can account for a much higher catch rate of common carp than mirrors? I think there is a very big chance of that being a reality. I personally love the majestic look of a big common carp, especially when they are mouth, fin, and scale perfect. I have been very fortunate in that I have caught some cracking looking commons over the years, from all types of waters. I think it all started with Richard Walker's record common from Redmire Pool all those years ago. After many years of playing around with different types of flavour bases and base mixes I think there could indeed be something in the idea that commons could be attracted to certain bases. I think there is an idea amongst some anglers that commons actually feed differently to their less scaly brethren. Well that may not be as far fetched as it sounds as I know at least three large waters where there are commons that are present that don't get caught. Possibly hooked and lost occasionally but not put on the bank. I have had discussions with other anglers who just dismiss the idea of there being a large uncaught common in some lakes as pure myth. The anglers in question don't know anything about the waters I am talking about. Especially as I know a particularly large common that was last caught at 39lb some seventeen years ago and has only been seen by a handful of very observant anglers since. One of those anglers had landed the biggest mirror in the lake at just over 48lb and some time later whilst wading in the shallows saw the fish he landed sitting with this huge common and said it dwarfed the mirror. It could easily have been low to mid 50lb in weight. Is that such an unbelievable thing to talk about? My mate Tappy who dives the lakes in question has indeed said he has seen an absolute pig of a common in another lake whilst diving, and actually said to me if you stuck a hook in that fish, you would know all about it. Take Fox Pool for instance where the knowledgable regulars, including Rob Maylin, thought that there were no more than a handfull of commons in there, mainly because they hardly ever got caught. When they drained the place how many were there in there? I think it was seventeen or so, and that was in a relatively small lake with an abundance of very good anglers fishing it. Makes you wonder, doesn't it? I know there was a large common in Larkfield after having spoken to a couple of anglers that had hooked and lost it. Very level headed anglers - not dreamers. Rocky (Roy Ashdown) caught a stunning common from Alders Lake years ago. It was almost orange in colour and I think over 35lb at the time. I hooked it and played it to the net with a witness at hand but the hook pulled and we reckoned that was not far short of 40lb. To my knowledge it hasn't been landed since and one of my mates now controls the fishing there so I get to know about the catches. That fish is unmistakable and would easily be recognised. The reason I labour the point here is that there are so many examples of big commons getting away with it. But are there things you can do to improve your chances of catching those fish? Well, possibly yes I think there is, I caught the Cotton Farm common in no time at all really and I caught a large common from the old Leisure Sport Sutton Lake which hadn't been out for about fifteen months. I caught possibly the biggest common in another syndicate lake at 46lb 12oz. I also had a very good year on Alders before moving on, all commons again, and incidently during my last year on Leisure Sport Sutton I never caught a mirror at all, just commons. Coincidence? I don't know but food for thought. All those commons were caught on exactly the same base chemical.

A lot of flavour companies use varying base chemicals. What one company uses to make a strawberry flavour is not necessarily the same as another company uses, or in fact the next one. That is what makes some flavours stand out from the crowd, take no notice of what we smell, because regardless of what we smell, it won't be the same to a carp. The chemical signals a fish picks up from a taste/

profile/smell/solubility will be totally different to our senses. I have used certain old type confectionery flavours that just keep on working time and time again. That takes years to find out about. Back in the seventies when we used Rayners food flavours (in Bull Lane), we had to work our way through sometimes up to six or seven types of food flavours of the same smell in order to find out the best one. There was a certain lemon flavour we used that was streets ahead of the others called 'lemon'. That was because of the concentration figures used in sorbets and out of all of them just that one showed higher concentration of solubility. There are bait experts out there that will tell you lemon is not a good flavour to use in a carp bait, whatever, tell that to the hundreds of carp that ended up in the bottom of our landing nets. There were two flavours that I used to blend together with an amino acid compound and that was second to none. Summer, winter, autumn it didn't matter, it worked on any water and as a label for a certain type of bait it really had no equal in my mind. The company that had made those two flavours was to close down, someone else took over and as much as I pleaded with them to make up the same batch, they couldn't, because the base ingredients were just no longer available. I was, and still am, gutted. I have tried for the last twenty years to track down the equivalent of those two and can't. I have received God knows how many samples from all over the place after bullshiting my way past company directors with promises of huge orders in the future, but it didn't matter, the end product wasn't there. There is a fashion at the moment to copy other company's flavours, buying a bottle of flavour from one company and giving it to a flavourist to duplicate, and they are convinced that they have the ideal copy. What a load of nonsense. I had a small bottle of a certain flavour which I called esterberry, it was alledgedly made up on a synthetic strawberry oil (is there such a thing) and contained esters. The result was outstanding, many of those I sold it to swore by it and secretly emptied waters with it, in the winter especially. That was from the same stable as the other two, and too became unavailable. I gave what I had left to an established flavour company and the owner swore that he could break down all the components, analyse all the ingredients and replicate the flavour. This company had been around for donkey's years and still supplies a large percentage of bait firms. What I got back was similar but not even remotely close to the original. John Baker's salmon was the same, God knows how many carp that flavour accounted for as a label. I used it in semolina/soya flour mixes and birdfood mixes, and in a LT94 mix with krill and soluble fish protein and couldn't believe the amount of fish we caught. What I am saying here is there are flavours that will turn fish on their heads. Ask Ritchie MacDonald how many fish that flavour accounted for, or Peter Springate, but if the company doesn't produce that flavour any more because they can't obtain the raw ingredients, then that's it. There is nothing you can do about it regardless of what someone says at a bait company. Just remember that there are far more carp anglers that get caught on certain products than carp. That, my friends, is a fact! And publicity has more to do with it than carp on the bank. I could write down a load of recipes that will help you to catch some carp but it's all been done before, and in this world of convenience carp fishing you will be far more tempted to buy your bait at an extortionate price than try and make your own bait. Bait is all about confidence - those that have spent the time learning to make their own bait will in my opinion always have a slight edge because they can be far more versatile in their approach, by way of what they use. Personally the group of guys I fish with have had our baits made for us by Tony at Premier this year because I trust his judgement, and know that he understands what we are trying to do. He also has some outstanding products and quality ingredients. Bait is all about confidence. You have to believe your bait will work, and stick with it. Don't change your bait every five minutes, that will achieve nothing I can assure you. I think the longest I have used the same bait for was eight years and that takes some doing but if the bait is good, then it will continue to work. Happy baiting . . .

February in freezing north east winds

January, they love thier bird foods

Chapter Thirteen

A Look at Rigs

Along with bait, this is another favorite subject of mine. Quite clearly there are times when even with the best going bait won't catch fish if you are fishing a water where the carp are tricky! By that I mean difficult to catch or, for want of a better word, clued up. Then your rigs can make a huge difference to how many fish you put on the bank, and how many you don't! Certainly on some of the waters I have fished over the last thirty years it is blatantly obvious that carp have been getting away with it. If I took notice of some of the things I have seen carp do to my hook baits over the years, I wouldn't bother fishing again. Nothing changes, it has been going on right under our noses, and will continue to do so for as long as there are carp and carp lakes.

Thirty years ago on the Johnson complex we were witnessing how the carp were coming into the swim, eating all the freebies and swimming off and leaving just our hook baits. So what do you think they are doing these days? In a word they are still getting away with it, only on a grander scale. I can't comment on anywhere else as ninety-five percent of my carp fishing has been done in Kent. I would say that since the very early sixties Kent has received more than its fair share of pressure, not so much so now but back then Kent held some of the biggest carp in the country, which in turn attracted some of the country's top anglers. This put more pressure on the fish, which in turn made the carp even harder to catch. It's called 'Danger by Association'. On the few, rare occasions I have fished in other counties it has become blatantly obvious that there has been nowhere near the amount of pressure on those waters by comparison to some that I have fished in my backyard. Along with very observant friends of mine we have witnessed just how easy it can be for carp to clear out all your free offerings and leave your hook baits all on their own. The worrying thing is that not all carp feed or test baits in the same fashion. No disrespect but I have never watched an underwater video on carp's reaction to bait, or rigs, nor have I any intention of doing so. It's never, ever stopped me catching carp! If you like watching underwater videos of STAGED situations, then good luck to you. Personally I prefer what happens in the real world by watching the reactions of the carp I am fishing for in the lake I am fishing. Larkfield was by far the best water I have ever fished where you could observe exactly just how the carp get away with disposing of your hook baits. Not only is the water crystal clear most of the time, but the carp can be as difficult to catch as any water I have ever fished. Sutton-at-Hone is on the same kind of level but most of the time you just can't see what is going on because of the lack of water clarity. You would think that would make it easier to conceal your end tackle, not so. There is only one person who ever made Sutton look easy and that was a bloke called Tony Stanley. That's right, you have never heard of him, but for my money, Tony made all the so-called superstars that fished Sutton past and present look like complete amateurs. I think Tony must have caught almost all of those Sutton carp three times over at least. That's not an exaggeration but a fact, and he wasn't a very well liked man. Well he wouldn't be as he caught more carp than anyone else by a mile. Personally I liked the man, he was an exceptional angler but I haven't heard of him for years, he may be dead I don't know. Having conversations with him when I was on there the first time round, made an awful lot of sense and it wasn't long before I realised why he caught so many. It was never really about his rigs as such, more his set up and how finely tuned it was. His rigs were quite simple but his indicator system in relation to his lead and terminal tackle was to him the most important part of it all. My old mate Ken Rowley achieved something similar when he fished the Darenth one winter back in the eighties; he was so consistent, more so than most on there at that time and he only fished from first light to about 3.30pm. He too balanced his lead and indicator set up in a similar way to Tony. A lot of anglers these days, certainly the ones I have come across where I have been fishing, do pretty much the same thing as other guys on the lake. But more of that later. Going back to Tony Stanley, some called him Hitler, I have no idea why but along with Steve Edwards they were the best two anglers I have ever come across. I can remember talking to Tony in the Gate swim at Sutton and we were discussing his approach. He was saying that he couldn't possibly compete with all the bait groups that were on Sutton at the time in terms of type of bait they were putting in, but he could compete with them in terms of quantity of the bait he was using. At that time I don't think there was a bait ban of any type on Sutton so Tony was using broken brazil nuts by the box load. The carp were indeed going potty on them, and to my knowledge he was the first person I ever knew who was using them at that time. I knew some guys who published their use on Yateley some years later but not then. On one occasion while we were talking, his tip pulled down towards the water's edge and just quivered. Tony said, "That's it, he's hung himself," and with that the buzzer screamed and Tony was in. To cut a long story short he landed a low thirty common which he just unhooked and slipped back into the lake. I laughed, "Are you not going to photograph that then?" "No mate," he said, "I've caught that particular common five times in the last two years." I laughed even more. No wonder some anglers on there at the time hated him. Personally I could see why he put it straight back, why would you want another picture of a fish you have caught that many times before? A lot of the anglers on there at that time said he was disrespectful to the fish by just putting them back without taking a picture of the catch. Personally I think they hated his success rate more than they hated what he was doing, as I never saw him once harm a fish. He always treated carp with the utmost respect. The reason I mentioned Tony Stanley is because it reinforces the belief that you can still fish a difficult water on your own and catch carp without having to be part of a bait group. What you do need, however, is to come up with a plan that is different to what is being used by the majority of anglers on your chosen water. You also don't always need to have a rig set up that looks like something from outer space in order to trick carp into picking up your hook bait. As I mentioned earlier I think the term 'danger by association' is a perfect title.

Carp can only relate to something that alarms them by the amount of times they get caught by the same situation. To put it in easier terms, if I went into a bar every night for a beer or two and each night a dirty great skinhead came over and punched me in the kisser, then eventually, as much as I like the beer and the fit barmaid, I am not going to go into that bar again, am I ? Or maybe I will, but not if the skinhead is in there! That kind of logic applies to carp fishing. In most lakes there are features of some kind or another, they are not new, and since time began carp have been getting caught on those features. Mainly this is because those features have always contained food of one source or another, be it natural or anglers' bait (unnatural). Once those carp have been caught on those features God knows how many times, they will no doubt treat those areas with extreme caution. This also means that your chances of tricking that carp on that feature for the umpteenth time is pretty remote ! Yet pick up any carp fishing magazine you like and within its pages you will find someone writing about the rewards of putting out a marker float and finding a feature, then spodding out your chosen feed to that marked spot. So much so that it is enough to send you to sleep. On a water I was fishing until about a year ago I would sit on the anti social bank and watch the events unfold and this is what I saw. A guy would go into a swim, get out his marker rod, cast around until he found what he was looking for then out comes the spod rod, and he proceeds to spod out whatever combination of food he has with him.He then casts out his rods onto the spot for the night. The next day he packs up, maybe he has caught one, but more often than not he hasn't. He leaves the swim and goes home. Then down comes another guy, goes into the same swim and does exactly what the previous bloke has done before him. It's so boring and repetitive that I am just senseless just writing about it. This procedure happens all the time. Even on the lake I am fishing now, which is rather hard, there are at least ten swims that see the same procedure every time I go down. In the autumn I was doing two midweek nights and the guys who turned up to do an overnight session repeated that situation time and time again of the bloke who had been in the swim the previous night. What does that tell you? It tells me that I want to be as far away from those swims as is humanly possible. Occasionally you may well benefit from dropping into a swim that has food going into it on a regular basis, but personally I think that the good times are far outnumbered by the times where you catch nothing. Look, carp know exactly what baits are! Especially those round things that everyone puts in the lake, it's been going on for almost fifty years and even the very best bait around will be treated with suspicion. Personally once I know a lake, or at least know what is roughly out in front of me, then the marker rod stays at home. I will only use the spomb rod if I am using a type of bait that I can't put out with a catapult. If there is a seagull problem, then I will bait up a little at night using the shadows to mark a chosen area. I honestly can't believe the number of blokes who sit on the bank firing out baits during the day, and all they are doing is feeding the seagulls. I have for at least the last fifteen years caught far more on one to ten bait stringers than I have on a patch of bait, or stuff I have put out in a spod or spomb. Personally I let the carp be my marker as honestly and truthfully I couldn't care less what the depth is in front of me, nor do I care if there is a feature in front of me. All I want to know is that there is a carp or two in front of me and that those carp are feeding. That is all I am interested in. I have also lost count of the number of times when anglers turn up in a swim and carp are crashing all over the place in front of the swim. What do they do? They get a marker rod out! Are you completely insane? Where on earth does that come from? I can only assume that they have read it in a magazine somewhere and that someone has suggested is the way to do it! That isn't the way to do it at all. Casting a marker rod out over feeding fish is the quickest way to invite those feeding carp to vacate your swim. Over the last, say, eight years I have had numerous multi catches of carp, by that I mean anything from two to seven carp in two to six hours. That's not because I am a better angler than those around me because I am not, it is because these days carp are under far more pressure than they have been for years. If you want to catch them, then you have to be on top of your game. All the best bait and rigs in the world are completely useless if you are fishing like a plank! Let's take a typical lake, say twenty acres, and you have about thirty swims on it. All of those swims receive an influx of bait. What is the difference between all of those swims? Nothing! There is no difference. They all have bait in, and at some point they will have carp in them. In today's carp fishing circumstances if you want to catch, you have to think.

Carp can swim around all day long and enter a swim and carefully eat a few baits from a patch of hundreds, then move to the next swim, and eat a few more baits, then onto the next swim so on and so forth. The more the swim gets topped up with bait, the more the carp get away with it. and the less chance you have of catching them. If I walk into a swim on a lake that is not pressured, then of course I will put a bit of bait in, but most of us don't fish those types of waters any more. They are a rarity, a real rarity. The waters you and I fish are waters that see a lot of anglers and a lot of bait and pressure. Take a swim on a typical lake, if there is such a thing. I would much rather have six baits round each hook bait, that is a seven to one chance of a take. If I put out two hundred baits then that is a 201/1 chance of a take. You don't need to be a gambler to work out those odds. Yes I know that lots of bait in a swim can work, but that's OK if you are a sponsored angler with five days a week to fish. But those people are in the minority. Look, unlimited time plus unlimited bait equals carp on the bank. I did that about ten years ago. The lake I was fishing at the time was, and still is, a pressured lake. I had very little work so I was going down the lake midweek and it was obviously quiet. I would turn up, fish an hour before first light until around 11.00am, then put in a kilo of bait and then go home. I would return the next morning, catch a couple of carp, put out more bait, go home, return the next morning, catch a couple more carp and so on and so forth. It was at that point that I realised if you put in time, effort and bait and you fish correctly, then you catch carp. It's a simple equation. But like most anglers, if you fish weekends and you are fishing at a time when the lake is under pressure, then you are going to struggle. More often than not, it's how you fish, and what you do that is different that can at difficult times catch you more fish. That is the whole point of this chapter. I mentioned earlier that I've been accused of being a fluky angler because of the very nice carp I have caught over the years. Some very large, some just plain stunning, and in a relatively short space of time. I am not a full time angler, and for as long as I can remember I have, like most of you out there, only fished on a Saturday night for about sixteen hours. If that makes me a fluky angler, then so be it. Like I said before, the blokes that usually accuse you of being fluky are the ones who suffer from green eye syndrome and who gives a toss about them anyway? Sometimes it is your rigs that can indeed make all the difference. Carp pick up baits and test baits all day long, and if what you do is different to the norm, then you can indeed trick the odd fish into picking up your hook bait. Larkfield taught me many things, just by watching those tricky old carp pick up and eject baits. It taught me that you have to be more than one jump ahead of the carp you are fishing for. In the crystal clear waters of Larkfield I learnt early on that not all carp feed in the same way, and maybe that is why some carp avoid capture for many years. From what I saw, it soon became apparent that some of the known carp fed completely differently to the ones that were seen on a regular basis and were not caught. There are those that say if a carp feeds on bait, then it will get caught! I certainly don't subscribe to that point of view from what I have seen. Here is a prime example. When Fox Pool, or Longfield as it was known, was drained, those that fished it said that there were only two or three commons in there. When they drained it there were around a dozen or more. What does that tell you? That they escaped capture, not only that but do we really know as much about carp fishing as we profess to know? I know very little about Fox Pool as I only fished it twice, but I do know about Larkfield as I was the head bailiff for around eight years. I pretty much covered the lake, either by boat or by wading round the margins, and some of the things I saw, along with my friends, would make your hair stand on end. There are many recountable tales about Larkfield, and I see no reason to believe it is any different, other than the size of fish, to other waters in the country where the carp are hard to catch. Like I said, I can only talk about the waters I have fished personally but Larkfield is like many of those waters that are hard to catch fish from. I would, like others I fished with, observe the carp's reactions to bait and some carp would drop down on your free offerings and pin them down to the lake bed. Then you would see them open their gills and suck! If the bait was a free offering, it would go back to the throat teeth and be eaten. If it was attached to a hook link, it would rattle about in the carps mouth and arouse suspicion so the carp would gently lift upwards and with its mouth open just upright itself and leave the hook link and bait there then swim off. Other times the carp would suck baits from inches away and because they were tethered to fixed rigs would straighten then fall short of the carp's mouth. Other times I have watched carp suck the hook bait into the mouth and if the hook caught on the inside of the carp's mouth, the carp would just suck and blow until the hook bait just fell out. Then it would swim off. When I fished Cotton Farm I saw the same thing. My mate Geoff Tarrant had a bait in the margins by some rushes in about three feet of crystal clear water and I was standing very close to the rushes in my chest waders in full view of Geoff's hook bait. A low thirty came into the area and was picking up his free offerings. When it came up to his hook bait it sucked it in and then obviously realising it had made a mistake it sat there and I watched in disbelief as it sucked and blowed until the hook fell out of its mouth. I could have said to Geoff, "Strike!" But I wanted to see what would happen in that situation. The carp ejected the bait. Geoff would never have known what was going on had I not told him, and that was some eighteen years ago. Do you think that carp fishing has advanced that much since then? I very much doubt it. Geoff never even got a single bleep on his buzzer. Do you think much has changed? No. I don't either. Most of the time if you are fishing out in the lake, you don't have a clue what is going on. No underwater DVD is going to change that, it is what it is. Sometimes you catch them, sometimes you don't. Personally I think it is your rigs and baiting situation that determine whether you catch during the scratching times! I have over the years tied up some ridiculous rigs in a futile effort to fool wary carp. Some have worked, some have not. My best mate Tony Tappenden remarks to me all the time that it's the greedy pig syndrome. When they are having it they are having it, the rest of the time you just have to try and outsmart them! How right is he? Over the years, most of the blokes who really know me will tell you that I will change my set up or rigs until I catch a fish. They are only carp and I don't believe they can get away with it for ever. The very first time I set eyes on Larky 2 was in the spring and to be perfectly honest I can't remember what year it was. Who cares, but I can remember getting down the lake after we had purchased our new tickets from LSA. It was around March time, and the fish were crashing all over. Ted Bryan, Graham Hackett and myself were set up in the swims from the Willows to the Back Point, and we had no end of Larky carp crashing all around - there were a lot of fish in front of us. Quite clearly they were feeding fish, but they were certainly not picking our hook baits up. I kid you not we had seen at least fifty show between first light and ten o'clock. I kept changing my hooklinks until I had a take, which eventually I did. That was a take on a three inch 1.5lb breaking strain nylon hair to a size ten hook, and a 10lb breaking strain hook link. I lost the fish to a hook pull, but at least I had managed a take, which was encouraging. Quite clearly Larkfield was not going to be a pushover water at all. We fished our socks off that first year, for very little reward. I personally only caught about three fish that first season. Interestingly enough I was at that time using Berkley Big Game line in a sandy color and definitely wasn't happy with it. Eventually I was put on to a line by Roy Ashdown (most people know him in this neck of the woods as Rocky), who was an exceptional young angler. Well he was then, now he is an exceptional older angler. Anyway the line he told me about was called Silver Thread, and it made a massive difference to our catch rate. The line lay was OK but I am convinced it was the actual invisibility of the line that made all the difference. It is the only line that I have ever used that made that much difference. I went from three fish to seventeen in my second season and I only fished on Saturday nights, so yes that was a result for Larkfield. Admittedly by this time I had started using the LT94 herring fishmeal in our baits so that, coupled with the Silver Thread line and the rigs we were using, made a massive difference. I expanded on the fishmeal situation in the bait chapter but it made a huge difference to our results. In terms of rigs, how long is a piece of string? Over the last thirty years at least, I have messed around with rigs. I have been shown some absolutely outrageous rigs that I would never, ever, repeat. More so because they were absolutely outrageous, unethical, beyond compare type rigs that I tried and thought were not fit for use in carp fishing. Kent has long been a melting pot of exceptional ideas, both on rigs and bait. Some of which I have had to wrestle with my conscience in order to try out, including self hooking rigs that really were not ethical in any shape or form. One rig that I was shown involved the use of a biro tube, high strength elastic, a small ring and pins. The outset of this was that once PVAd up it was like a mouse trap that sprung and pulled the hook into the fishe's mouth so hard that the takes you had were absolutely violent. So much so that I questioned the ethical reason for the use of it. I caught about fifteen fish in a week using that rig and my concerns were that the shocks of being hooked in such a violent nature were indeed grounds not to use it. I honestly felt that a carp could possibly do itself damage from such a shock to the system. I actually watched a carp trigger the rig in the margins and absolutely freak out before screaming off out into the lake at a rate of knots that left me in no doubt that the rig would remain unused by me. I never used it again. My carp fishing is about enjoyment, not carp at any costs. There was another rig invented in Kent that was called the Sputnik rig, which was another totally outrageously unethical rig involving pins. That was even worse in the bolt rig stakes. The scary thing is that it shows just how far some anglers will go in order to put fish on the bank with absolutely no regard to the carp's welfare. So before all you budding rig inventers run away with the idea that what you are doing is unique, don't, there are very few rigs around that have not been used before. The stiff rig was used during the seventies to stop bite offs - we used 30lb breaking strain sea fishing line to stop fish ejecting the hook bait. Or, it was meant to make them bolt when fishing over particles. Those types of rigs were designed to be frighteners. The so called KD rig was one we used on Larkfield maybe twenty years ago or more. No disrespect to Kenny Dorsett - he is a fantastic angler but that rig isn't new. I know Steve Edwards used it with three turns up the shank and four turns behind the hair, making the hair stick out and offset the hook at a funny angle. I personally used a lead shot on the hair just below the bait on Johnson's over twenty years ago landing tench of 9lb 12oz and 10lb 6 oz. They were big tench back then and a darn sight smarter than the carp. Very few rigs are unique, in my humble opinion. The only true rig that really turned carp fishing on its head was Kevin Maddocks and Len Middleton's hair rig. Now that really was a huge breakthrough. I personally don't think that there has been anything like it since but just mediocre theories on a theme. The bent hook rig and the 360 rig certainly do what is required in order to hook fish. I used both of those rigs for a while but I am afraid that the damage I saw to carp's mouths made me feel sick. I personally double hooked several carp on both of those rigs so I stopped using them. I also help cut out hooks from carp's mouths with scalpels and wire cutters on the Tip Lake at Darenth. Phil, one of the boys on my bait, landed a fish called Wades Wonder, and that fish had two other hooks in its mouth. Both bent hooks. One was double hooked and covered in newly grown flesh and the other was double hooked and pinning one side of the carp's mouth together. Like I said we had to cut both hooks out and treat the fishe's mouth with antiseptic. I read a piece in a weekly magazine not too long ago where the consultant/author, Andy Maker was saying that a lot of damage to carp's mouths was caused by small hooks used by match anglers or coarse anglers when the carp were young! Really? I think most of us in the real world realise that carp with torn, ripped or damaged mouths is the direct result of anglers who not only use dodgy or unsafe rigs but also bully fish. Only two months ago at the time of writing this chapter (December 2011) Tony Tappenden and I had taken a walk round a lake to see an old mate of ours who was fishing. Another bloke walked into the swim who our mate knew. This bloke started spouting off about a trip he had just got back from in France and was bragging it. He came straight out with, "It is amazing how much stick you can give carp. We were turning those fish over on their backs. I even snapped a (he then mentioned a name of a hook) in half on a fish!" I just walked away. With clowns like that in carp fishing its no wonder carp's mouths get damaged, and it's got sod all to do with carp being caught when they were young! SORRY, but some things have to be said. They may not be nice but there are indeed clowns like that in carp fishing now and that's why I keep as far away from them as possible. I have absolutely nothing in common with a percentage of modern day carp anglers who fish to put carp on the bank at any cost. Sorry, I had to get that off my chest! If you look at rigs nowadays, most of them involve the use of baits tied close to the shank of the hook. But quite clearly the main advantage of hook and bait is separation. If you achieve that, you have a rig that is hard to eject. Once again Larkfield was indeed a great place to learn how to outsmart fish because you could see everything that they were doing to your hook bait. I think personally that most of the successful rigs I have come across have been so successful because they are simple. I've seen some rigs published that are just plain ludicrous, rings, swivels, bits and pieces all over the place. There was a rig

I saw in a magazine that I tried to tie up myself and I struggled big time. It took ages and I've been fishing for donkey's years. The rig involved a couple of rings that were connected to a pop-up and was meant to slide freely, but the minute you dropped it anywhere near weed, (Larkfield can be full of at times) the whole thing was useless. Maybe the rig did work in crystal clear water but not where I was fishing. In fact most of the rigs I used on Larkfield that involved a bait that was very tight to the hook shank never really caught me anything. Almost all the fish I caught on Larkfield were either on a two to three inch 1lb 10oz double strength nylon hair, nylon hook link on a running lead set up. Or on a two inch multi- strand hooklink fished as a sliding bolt rig type set up incorporating a six inch backstop. I did have a couple of fish on what I called a double barrelled rig. I don't know where that came from, I just started using it after watching carp in Larkfield upend over hook links and trap the link to the lake bed. They would then suck and obviously if the bait was unsafe, it would just rattle around in the mouth. Then the carp would slowly upright itself leaving the hook bait on the bottom. I have to say that carp were testing baits in so many different ways that it was somewhat confidence sapping. I will get onto the reasons as to why I have used some of the rigs and explain each one. I have to explain that I have used some quite strange set ups but they have all caught me carp. At times those rigs have produced some of the biggest carp in the lakes I have fished at the time. Like most anglers I only do one nighters, so I want to put myself in a position whereby I give myself the best chance of catching a carp or two in the time I have at my disposal. Sometimes you have to just try and do something different to what is going on around you.

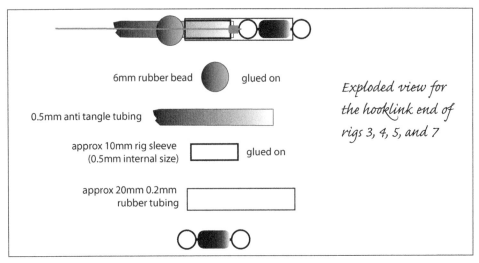

6mm rubber bead   glued on

0.5mm anti tangle tubing

approx 10mm rig sleeve   glued on
(0.5mm internal size)

approx 20mm 0.2mm
rubber tubing

Exploded view for the hooklink end of rigs 3, 4, 5, and 7

RIG 1. Sliding Shock Rig

Originally one of my mates since schooldays, Colin Cameron, had put a rig together when we were on the same lake together. It involved the use of an inline lead that slid freely over a fifteen inch length of stiff anti tangle tubing. Basically you cast out, the lead hits bottom and the tube then lays flat. The carp picks up your hook bait, and as the carp rights itself it lifts the lead. The lead then slides down the tubing, smacking into the bit of lead wire at the end of the anti tangle tubing that he used to keep the tubing laying flat. It had a bit of a shock effect and the takes were quite positive. Personally I thought Colin's idea was a great idea, but I also felt that it could be massively improved. I never really gave the rig much more thought until I fished the Darenth complex, where some of the fish were getting pretty cute regarding rigs. What I wanted was something far more supple and free running - relatively tangle free. I only intended to fish the rig in the margins at maybe fifteen yards out at a push. So my version used a six to seven inch length piece of 0.5 mm soft anti tangle tubing. I glued a small rubber bead onto one end. I then slid on an inline lead which had stiff anti tangle tubing glued on the inside of the lead. Once that was on I slid on another rubber bead, which would be used as a buffer for casting. After this I slid on a piece of valve rubber that was glued up against the rubber bead. On top of that was a piece of 2.5mm silicone that would house the swivel, held just enough to pop out and become free running once the carp was pricked and swam off when it hit the backstop. The biggest issue with any rig I make or use is 'safety'. My conscience has to be clear that if I get cut off, crack off or the line parts for any reason, then I have to be confident in the knowledge that the fish has left all my tackle on the bottom of the lake bed. The only thing it has to get rid of is the hooklink. I must at this point say that is why I make my own rigs. At one time I used the so-called safety lead clips for about three months when they first came out. I honestly have never used them since; I wouldn't give them house room. Just about every tethered carp I have seen landed or landed myself has been towing either lead core, or a lead clip. So for that reason alone I won't use them. If you look at the rig itself, it should be obvious as to why I put it together. It is a confidence rig. At the time I had seen fish picking up baits and ejecting them straight away. Sometimes the hook held but on a short hair, more often than not the hook just followed the bait out without catching in the mouth. On a very long hook link, which was all the fashion at the time, the carp would sometimes back off and as soon as it felt any resistance, would just stop, and suck and blow until the hook got dislodged and was ejected. What I wanted to achieve was to use a multi strand hook link that was very short, no more than two inches maximum. The idea being that because the hook link was so supple, the carp wouldn't feel the strands on its bottom lip. I used a very light, wide gape hook with this rig, ironically when I tied it up, I tied it with 3 turns up the shank then 4 turns behind the hair to make the multi strand hair fold back at an odd angle. (This was thirty years ago and I never invented that knot. But apparently it's all the rage now and only just been invented). On ejection the bait would be pulling against the eye that would cause separation of hook and bait and the force of ejecting the bait would pull the hook home. Then the carp would swim off and bang straight into the back stop and the swivel would pop out of the silicone and bingo, game over, a full bloodied run would occur. I always fish this set up with a bow in the line and with plenty of slack from the rod tip. Nine times out of ten with this set up you get a single bleep then an absolute ripper. I kid

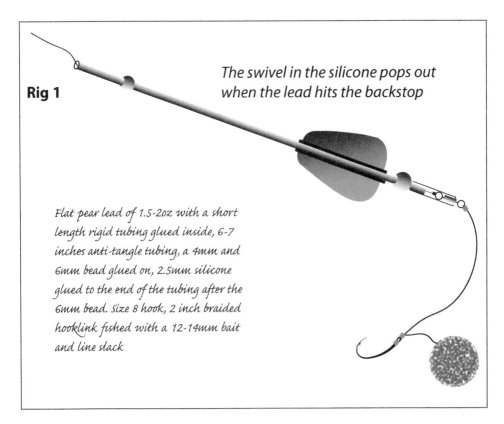

Rig 1

The swivel in the silicone pops out when the lead hits the backstop

Flat pear lead of 1.5-2oz with a short length rigid tubing glued inside, 6-7 inches anti-tangle tubing, a 4mm and 6mm bead glued on, 2.5mm silicone glued to the end of the tubing after the 6mm bead. Size 8 hook, 2 inch braided hooklink fished with a 12-14mm bait and line slack

you not. This rig still works a treat on waters where the carp are tricky to catch. I caught fish on this set up on Larkfield, Sutton-at-Hone, and Darenth. It was while fishing Larkfield that I foolishly showed Danny Fairbrass the rig in the local tackle shop. The next I knew it was published in his rig booklet the next year. In fairness to him he did credit me for the rig, but I think what was somewhat insulting was that the cheeky young pup said that he felt I had it all wrong and the rig would be better used with nylon! I find that rich coming from a bloke who to my knowledge had never fished Larkfield and had no idea at that time why I put the rig together, or in what situation I was using it, but that's typical of some tackle manufacturers. Take someone's idea and flog it without knowing too much about it.

RIG 2. The Double Barrel Rig

The double barrel rig. I don't know where this rig came from. It's something I tried out on Larkfield because I had seen carp pinning hook links to the lake bed and it was the only way I could see of getting round the problem. I think Rod Hutchinson had written about the concertina rig which involved pulling a length of silicone tubing up a soft hook link material then letting it be drawn into the silicone as the silicone went back. There was also the extending hook link, two hook links that sat parallel to one another joined by Drennan rings and PVAd together and cast out. Like I said, I don't think I invented it but it must have come from somewhere. As

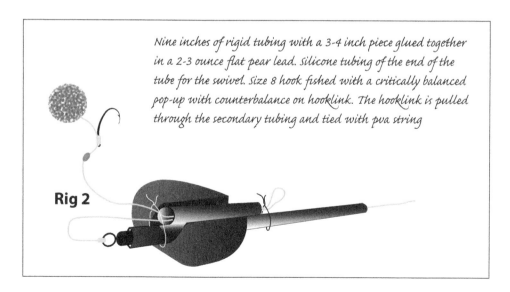

Nine inches of rigid tubing with a 3-4 inch piece glued together in a 2-3 ounce flat pear lead. Silicone tubing of the end of the tube for the swivel. Size 8 hook fished with a critically balanced pop-up with counterbalance on hooklink. The hooklink is pulled through the secondary tubing and tied with pva string

Rig 2

you can see from the drawing you glue two bits of stiff anti tangle tubing together laid into the inline lead, so you can put a baiting needle through, pull the hook link back through the tube and tie it up with PVA string using a critically balanced popup. One suck on the hook bait and it flies back into the carp's mouth regardless of whether the carp clamps its mouth over your lead or main line. The hooklink itself is contained in the tubing prior to the carp sucking on the bait. I only ever use this rig in the margins as it is far better to place such a set up on a marginal shelf. A word of warning - if you were to use this set up, then please make sure you use it with a short hook link, say six inches maximum, as the last thing you want is to have a carp suck the bait up on a long hook link and find it has shot up to the throat teeth or thereabouts. A deep hooked carp is NOT what you want.

RIG 3. The Long Hair Rig

This is self-explanatory and it's nothing new. It's been used since Kevin Maddocks and Lenny Middleton invented it. Its just a variation on a theme, but like everything else you do, just because it's considered old hat, that doesn't make it useless, nor does it make it ineffective. It is all relevant to where you are fishing. Personally I think this set up works so much better when you have the carp on a bait they want to eat but they are just very wary of picking up. The long, very light hair is very difficult to detect and allows the hook bait to react in a far more natural way than all your short hook links which rely on the hook turning in the carps mouth or on ejection in order to prick the fish. Loads of people have used this set up to great effect over the years. Dave Lane, among many on Horton, fairly emptied the place on this set up. What does surprise me though is the amount of people who I have seen use this set up and get their indicator set up completely wrong. When I was on Larkfield, there was one bloke who was using a twelve inch long hook link and a three inch hair, but instead of using a completely free running set up he had it fishing on a fixed inline lead. He couldn't work out why every time he wound back his hair had been snapped. Well just in case you too don't get it either the set up is a confidence rig. You need as much line free running as possible to allow the carp to suck the bait into the mouth. Once the carp feels the bait is safe it will take the bait back to the throat teeth but if your hook link is straight, then has no play in the line. All that happens then is that the hook stays outside of the carp's mouth and as the carp swims off the hair snaps. That is exactly what happened to matey on Larkfield, time and time again. I did try to help him and tell him why it was happening, but I just don't think he got it! You can only try! There have been many anglers who have written over the years about how they firmly believe that it is the lead that sets the hook but personally I don't subscribe to that theory in any shape or form. While I was on Larkfield I had carp move 4oz and 5oz leads as far as two feet away from where I placed them. All I received was one single bleep during the night. Have you ever watched your line when you have had a pull up on the indicator and you can see the fish on the end of the line moving parallel to you but not taking line - just moving in an arc. Admittedly it's not a regular occurrence but over say the last twenty years I have had it happen to me about a dozen times. If carp can do that, then they can move heavy leads without you knowing it. As recently as a month ago, (at the time of writing, December 2011) I had that happen to me. A fish pulled up my indicator no more than an inch, it then dropped an inch, all on a running lead set up. I had put that rod straight out but on deciding to pull into the fish it was a good thirty-five yards to my right and only about ten yards from a bed of dense rushes. Had I not worked out what the fish was trying to do, it would have been in the rushes and I probably would have lost it. I never take anything for granted these days; expect the unexpected if you want to put carp on the bank.

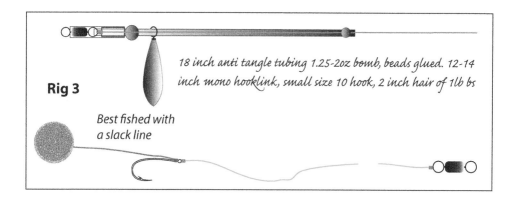

Rig 3

18 inch anti tangle tubing 1.25-2oz bomb, beads glued. 12-14 inch mono hooklink, small size 10 hook, 2 inch hair of 1lb bs

Best fished with a slack line

RIG 4. The Long Hooklink and Swivel Hook Rig

I quite often use excessively long hook links, for no other reason than to get the hook bait as far away from the lead as is humanly possible. Ironically it is the only short hair rig I use, but that is because it is different to most rigs you see. There are many anglers out there that write about the benefits of the hook turning in the mouth so that it catches, and all the time you see diagrams of a hand in the picture and how the hook turns over the hand and catches in the skin. Well tell me when was the last time was you saw a carp with hands? Sorry but I fail to see the significance of it. When a rig is underwater there is no way it will react in the same manner as when you run it across your hand in fresh air. Every time I tie up this set up the hook catches on everything it touches, that is all I am interested in, I couldn't care less what some expert or consultant writes about in his magazine feature because this setup puts carp on the bank for me. In fact this set up accounted for the Cotton Farm common on my third trip back on the water after years of being away from it. Maybe that's just another fluky catch. I fish a four inch back stop on a lot of the rigs I use, and this is no different. The Cotton Farm common was hooked four inches back in the mouth and all I could see was the eye of the hook when I unhooked it. That's all I need to know.....the rig worked.

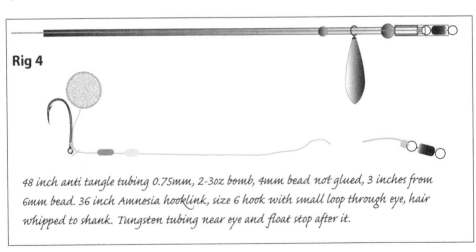

Rig 4

48 inch anti tangle tubing 0.75mm, 2-3oz bomb, 4mm bead not glued, 3 inches from 6mm bead. 36 inch Amnesia hooklink, size 6 hook with small loop through eye, hair whipped to shank. Tungsten tubing near eye and float stop after it.

Rig 5. The Blow Back Rig with a Three Inch Backstop

Once again, nothing groundbreaking here other than, like every rig I use, it doesn't involve the use of the so-called safety lead clip. I use an incredibly sharp hook with this set up, which I was put on to by Peter, the manager at the Tackle Box in Dartford. I know he comes from Essex, but that's not his fault. He is a genuine geezer who is always straight with me. He is a forward thinking angler, plus I have known him since he was a young pup when he worked in Specialist Tackle in Romford. I know, it's Essex again but you have to make allowances for that mob that live the other side of the river. Or, maybe its because I just like the bloke. Anyway the hooks I use with this set up are called Smart hooks and that is quite ironic considering who put me on to them! The set up involves a simple blow back rig using the Smart hooks in size 8 with the regulation small ring, long hair and back stop set up. I have caught about eighty-five percent of my fish in the last eight to ten years on this set up and that should tell you how much I value this set up. Most reliable and consistently successful rigs are usually quite simple in their make up. Every angler I know that puts more than their fair share of carp on the bank sticks to the basics of rig construction. This is no different, possibly the only thing I prefer is quite a long hair; once again separation is everything in my opinion. The further you get your hookbait apart from your hook the more there is a chance of pricking the inside of the carp's mouth when it ejects it.

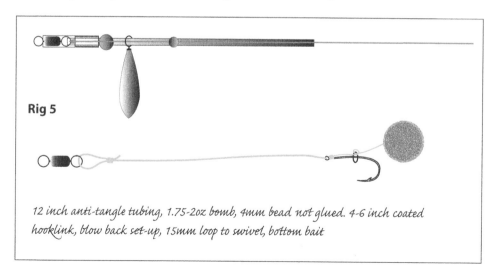

Rig 5

12 inch anti-tangle tubing, 1.75-2oz bomb, 4mm bead not glued. 4-6 inch coated hooklink, blow back set-up, 15mm loop to swivel, bottom bait

Rig 6. The Curved Hook Back Stop Rig

Again nothing special but highly effective with a back stop set up, especially when fished over hemp, chopped or souped bait. I had my best season on Alders Lake using this setup. That particular season an awful lot of people were fishing at range, when I say range I mean seventy yards plus, and a lot were at one hundred yards plus. This of course is their prerogative. I have fished long distance at times, sometimes around one hundred and thirty yards, that's range enough for me. It's OK for a while, but I find it incredibly boring and non educational. By that I mean you don't learn anywhere near as much fishing at that range, you are just there because you see fish there. I know anglers that only fish at range and refuse to fish close, even when the carp are dancing their socks off forty yards out. Good luck to them if that's what they enjoy. I am sure that some people are convinced that carp only feed at one hundred yards plus. Personally I have always believed that the margins are the biggest gravel bar in the lake, or biggest feature, whatever you want to call it. That particular season I had noticed that, because most anglers were trying to out cast each other to the middle of the lake, if you really looked you could see fish being very careful, feeding very close to the bank. Very seldom did you see them show during the day, they would be quite happy to poke their heads gently after dark, but even then you had to look. I think that's a classic sign of a pressured water. Maybe it's in my head but there are a lot of anglers these days that just don't seem to notice clear signs that carp are feeding close by, just a handful of bubbles, the odd swirl, weed beds just slightly swaying, tell-tale signs that carp are there in front of you and probably feeding.

I had found a very small bar, no more than thirty feet out from the bank, nine to ten feet of water all round but four to five feet of water on top of the bar. The bar was quite small, no more than two foot six wide and approximately twelve feet long, but enough room to put three rods on it. At that time I was using a particular process of cooking the hemp I was using, it wasn't my idea, I was told about it by Secret John's brother, Chris, as it wasn't my idea I have no place in telling you what that process was. He asked me at the time not to say anything, so I won't ! To cut a long story short, I introduced the processed hemp little and often to the little bar.

Chris did say to me to be careful not to put too much hemp out, as the process forces the oil out of the hemp and, being quite dense it sinks into the lake bed and carp will continue to return to the area long after the hemp has all gone. This proved to be spot on, one session I was at one end of the lake, and Chris was at the other end, I was only doing the night as I had to be off the next morning bright and early to take my son to football. I had only put out half a kilo over my three rods, but Chris who planned to do two, possibly three, nights had put out about four kilos of the processed hemp. About two hours after he had put the stuff out carp started showing over his patch. They were going potty. I think he had two or three fish in about an hour, and quite rightly so was settled in for major hauling, when disaster struck! He received a call from home telling him to get his backside home rapid as there was a family crisis. He had no option but to pack up and leave a swim with God knows how many carp in it that were going potty on his processed hemp. He called me on the jolly old mobile saying, "You have to get yourself over here and sit on the swim for a couple of days mate because if someone else goes in here, they will empty the place." I was completely gutted, I explained that I had to be gone early in the morning as one of my sons had a cup final match. To miss that would be like a death sentence for me! He left the lake absolutely pig sick, even as he packed his gear into the van carp were throwing themselves out of his swim one after the other. Don't you just hate it when that happens? That night a guy moved into the swim vacated by Chris, let's just call him Pieman, he sat there all weekend and landed around fourteen carp or so. As you can imagine by the time he left on the Sunday his gonads were indeed the size of melons. His claims of his new bait being the dog's nuts were indeed of legendary proportions, and he stood there with his chest puffed out like a peacock on heat!

I had to tell Chris what had happened and how many fish the God-like angler had caught over his patch of processed hemp, and the silence on the other end of the phone was deafening. Gutted is not the word I would have chosen. Do you know we kept tags on the amount of fish that were caught from that swim over three weeks and it was something like thirty-seven. Those carp just kept going back to that area for what was in the surrounding silt, and it wasn't bloodworm!

Some things in carp fishing are not always what they seem. Back to the plot, I continued to fish that bar for a few weeks and continued to catch. I think the best night I had was six fish to 36lb. The situation was quite amusing though, I would be fishing Saturday nights as I always did, and I caught every Saturday night. I always fished completely slack lines as people would walk round and as some do, they would look to see where you were fishing or where your lines were pointing. If the lines are just hanging off your rod tips, they haven't got a clue, and I would always cast an empty spodfull or three during the daylight hours, about sixty yards past where I was fishing, just to give the impression I was fishing further out. It is called the 'Kent Swerve'. I would walk round on some mid week evenings to find not just one bloke in the swim, but twice there were two blokes doubled up in the swim I had caught from. Their lines nice and tight not even touching the water for twenty-five yards. How sad is that? I must confess that on many occasions I really wanted to say, "Sorry lads but you are about forty-five yards out too far!" But who am I to spoil the swim slugs' fun?

Like many things in carp fishing, it can be very difficult to pinpoint exactly why a particular method, combined with a particular rig, and particular baiting situation works. Sometimes it's the whole combination of things on that particular water at that particular time. It can do your crust in if you try and analyse it, so my advice would be, don't. Just enjoy your fishing for the moment; I honestly don't know why I did so well that season. I was using 10mm bright pink pop-ups over the processed hemp, with very short hook links, and completely slack lines, allowing the backstop to set the hook against the lead. I was fishing no more than fifteen yards out anywhere on the lake that season, at a time when the fish were being pounded at range. Was it the pink hook bait fished over a bed of black food source that must have stuck out like a brand new tanner up a coal miner's arse!?Or was it that the carp were under no pressure in the margins because most of the blokes on there at that time just left the margins alone? I really don't know. I just do what I do. Sometimes it works and sometimes it doesn't. But with every lake I fish I will do my utmost to fish the complete opposite way to what the majority are doing.

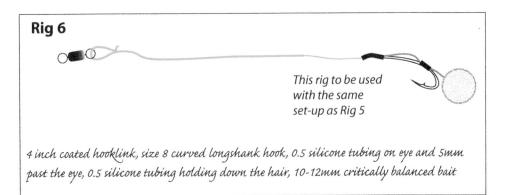

Rig 6

This rig to be used with the same set-up as Rig 5

4 inch coated hooklink, size 8 curved longshank hook, 0.5 silicone tubing on eye and 5mm past the eye, 0.5 silicone tubing holding down the hair, 10-12mm critically balanced bait

Rig 7. The Running Pop-Up Rig

Again nothing revolutionary about this rig, apart from the fact that just about every pop-up rig I see in a magazine is all about fishing a pop-up on a safety lead clip, a length of lead core, sinking leader, or a chod rig. Most of the time it's all about a pop-up tethered to a hook link either as a blow back set up on a ring at the back of the shank, whatever! I have read reports that people have watched carp pick up a chod rig and really struggle to get off the rig. Well this set up is very similar, in that once it's in the mouth the separation between the hook and bait is good, and the angle of the hook is savage, which aids hooking potential. Normally this is fair and square in the bottom lip. Every take I have had on this set up has been an absolute screamer although it looks like it's out of the ark in terms of modern day all singing, all dancing rigs that are supposed to be the dogs. I remember seeing Jim Shelley publish this rig, but I know for a fact that anglers in Kent have been using dental floss or something similar tied to the hooklink to fix a lead shot to for around thirty years. This was mainly because back in the day when we put lead shot on the hooklink to counter balance a pop up, nine times out of ten if a fish went through weed the lead shot would cut straight through the braided or nylon hook link. It was the weakest point of contact where the shot had been crushed on the line.

As you can see, once I cast out the rig and tubing, I drop on a floating back lead set up. This can be made to fish over any depth of weed by using a lead, usually I use half to three quarters of an ounce glued into stiff anti tangle tubing with Araldite. Model shops usually sell this as I think this kind of product is far too old hat to sell in tackle shops any more. Then you decide what length you want the stiff anti tangle tubing to be. Most of the time I use about six to eight inches of it. Then you drill out a half inch cork or polystyrene ball and thread it down on the tubing. The top two inches of tubing is heated, then let it fold over so it leaves a kind of rounded angle. Then when you slide up your cork, or poly ball it traps your line in the fold. Bingo, drop it in the drink and you can lift your rod and the floating back lead will gently go out as far as you want it to. Let it sink and bingo you have a free running set-up that the carp just can't get off. Once the line is sunk I tend to not bother with indicators, just pull tight to your lead then ease off about six inches of line to just slightly slacken your line to a kind of bow in the line. Sorted, they don't stand a chance. I know its not a state of the art rig with all new lovely components but it does what it was designed to do - put fish on the bank !

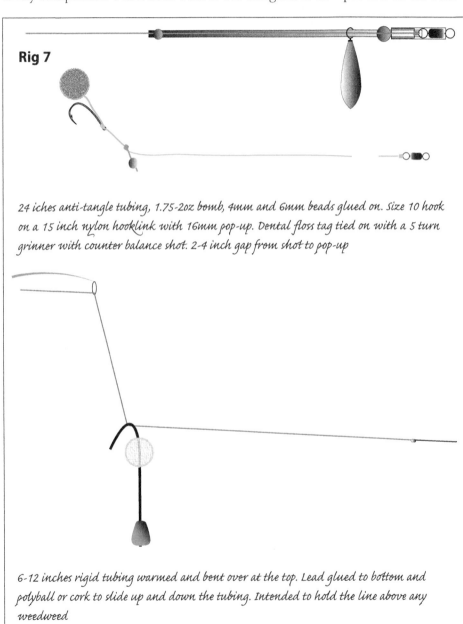

Rig 7

24 iches anti-tangle tubing, 1.75-2oz bomb, 4mm and 6mm beads glued on. Size 10 hook on a 15 inch nylon hooklink with 16mm pop-up. Dental floss tag tied on with a 5 turn grinner with counter balance shot. 2-4 inch gap from shot to pop-up

6-12 inches rigid tubing warmed and bent over at the top. Lead glued to bottom and polyball or cork to slide up and down the tubing. Intended to hold the line above any weedweed

8. The Floater Cake Rig

I would hazard a guess that eighty-five percent of anglers these days wouldn't even know what a floater cake is, let alone how to fish it. Obviously the world of modern day carp fishing has become obsessed with either mixer fishing with controllers or plastic baits fished zig rig style. Once again sorry to rain on the inventor's parade but the zig rig, as it is now called, was being used in the 60s. I know many people, including myself, who used that set up over forty years ago now, whilst using floating crust at varying depths. It only became really special once Fred Wilton invented his floater cake method. This was based on using his bottom bait recipe but using double the eggs and flavour levels plus a teaspoonful of baking powder. It was then baked in the oven for approximately one and a quarter hours and bingo you have, in my opinion, the best form of floating bait ever invented. And what is an even bigger bonus is that it is tailored to be exclusive to you. Your base mix and your choice of label (by that I mean flavour) and you can fish it anyway you want. Given the option of using lumps of foam cut in bits and odd bright colours or using a food source that carp are eating off the bottom all day long, only in a completely different format than they are used to. Then give me floater cake every single time! A prime example was way back when my friends and I were fishing the Tip Lake on the Darenth complex. Every one on there was mixer mad, box after box of chum mixers were being chucked in. At that time we were using the original Ian Booker Robin Red mix, which the carp were loving anyway, but I started making up a Robin Red floater cake mix, and because the Tip Lake was very weedy anyway it was perfect for fishing floater cake. The most important point here is that the carp in the Tip Lake probably hadn't seen floater cake for over fifteen years minimum, if not longer. I suspected they went absolutely potty on it, bearing in mind that they had been inundated with mixers for years. The reaction to floater cake was incredible, the carp kept charging at the one inch square bits of floater cake like demented dolphins, rising right up and with their heads out of the water they were desperately trying to gulp down the bits of cake whilst slurping away like crazy in order to eat every last bit. I firmly believe that, being as they had been subjected to years of eating mixers and dog and cat biscuits, they just couldn't deal with big square bits of floater. My only regret was that I hadn't started to introduce the floater cake sooner as it was then September and the weather started to change. It got much colder and things started to slow down. Never mind, there is always next year. While we are on the subject of so-called zig rigs, I have included a set up that was very popular on the Darenth Complex at the time but was kept firmly under wraps as it was devastating in terms of fish caught at varying depths. I have no idea who first came up with the idea, it may have been one of The Mental Squad boys that I fished with, but it was an incredibly successful method. Ironically I have never seen this rig in print anywhere either in a magazine or book. When I have mentioned it to the odd person they have always said that is a great idea, and that they have never seen it before. The first person who showed it to me was Gary Prosser, who had been emptying the Big Lake using it. The major advantage of using this set up over a standard pop-up off the lead was that the rig allows you to have three to four inches of movement when the carp sucks at the suspended pop-up. Once the hook is in the carp's mouth then its game over because the line is then connected straight to the lead and no matter what happens the carp feels the full weight of the lead and pulls the hook home. Job done. You can vary the depth of hook link to suit your fishing. He knew all chances of a take off the bottom had gone. He used to fish four feet off the bottom for an hour or two, then six feet off the bottom, then eight feet by lunchtime. All of this would

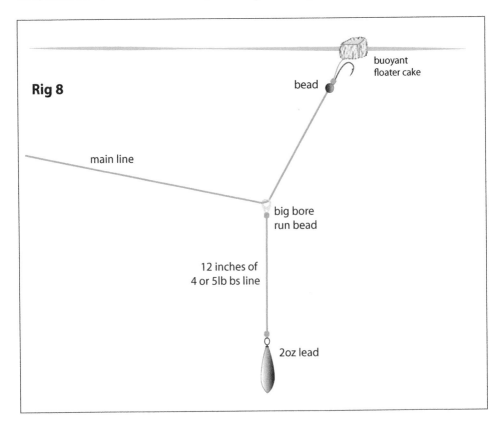

then be reversed to get lower in the water as evening approached. It was back to bottom baits for the night and early morning, unless it was very warm, when he would just leave them out all night at varying depths, The main feature of this set up is that you slide the tungsten tubing up close to your hook and pop-up. Then you trim the tungsten tubing until your hook bait is perfectly critically balanced. Then slide it back up to within three or four inches from your swivel, and just wait for the takes. This was indeed over thirty years ago. Once again, hands up anyone who thinks they invented the zig rig in the last ten years?. Another set up I used to good effect was the paternoster pop-up rig, which again you can fish at any depth, and the line drawing will explain it easily enough. If you are wondering how you cast out these kind of rigs to prevent the hook catching on anything on the cast, just do what the Darenth boys did At first I couldn't understand why The Mental Squad boys all had dirty great mugs for their tea, but all was revealed when I watched Dave Lawrence put his hook bait in the mug before casting out safely into the lake . . . very smart these Kent boys.

Rig 9. The No Name Rig

You may well have seen this rig in the angling press over the last couple of years but it was being used in Kent on waters like Sutton-at-Hone, the Johnson complex, Larkfield, Barden Park, just to name but a few. I kid you not when I say that we used this rig over twenty years ago. I personally caught tench to 10lb 6oz on it from Johnson, Larkfield, and God knows how many carp on it from Barden Park. I know that Steve Edwards was using it on Sutton-at-Hone, as well as other waters he was fishing. No offence to anyone claiming to have invented this rig in the last few years, but actually you didn't!

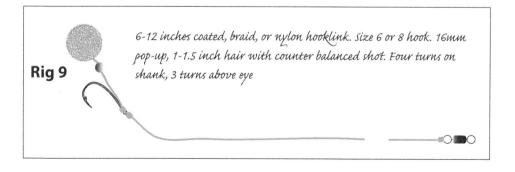

Rig 9

6-12 inches coated, braid, or nylon hooklink. Size 6 or 8 hook. 16mm pop-up, 1-1.5 inch hair with counter balanced shot. Four turns on shank, 3 turns above eye

10. The Weed Rig

This rig is a very effective set up for fishing in weed. I first used it on Redmire back in 1983. It is pretty self-explanatory. At the time Ken Rowley and I were using Black Spider right through on the spools, for two reasons. Firstly we had noticed that the carp in Redmire Pool were really spooky around lines, plus because of the weed in the pool, which could at times be almost unfishable, you just couldn't put a lead out into a clear spot without having tight line draped across any gaps in the weed. The Black Spider sank like a brick and draped itself all over any undulations in the weed or the lake bed so you could present a bait anywhere. The only issue was that because once wet the Black Spider was so heavy you couldn't cast it far, maybe twenty yards or so, but who cares? Like a lot of waters that become heavily weeded the carp were feeding in the margins most of the time, but even if they weren't, Redmire is only small so even if you could only cast twenty yards, you weren't far from the middle anyway. The weed in Redmire was quite strange as it would grow up in areas and then kind of collapse so it resembled a pile of candy floss. It was all uneven and you could clearly see the carp feeding on the top of it. Trouble was how on earth do you present a hookbait on top of that lot? Well with a lead you can't! But it dawned on me that if you tied on a swan shot every twelve inches to your braid, then not only would your hook bait (if you used a pop-up) stay in line and presentable but the whole length of braid between your chosen length of shots would indeed all sink at the same time . . . equilibrium I call it. I personally would tie on six swan shots at twelve inch intervals, which was enough weight to cast anywhere. Even in weed or on the uneven lake bed it would in fact

Braided main line, size 8 hook, 14mm pop-up. Five or 6 swan shot on dental floss tails 12- 15 inches apart attached with 5 turn grinners. Burn the ends to hold the shot

Rig 10

pin down your whole length of braid to your hookbait. The very first carp I caught on that set up was one of the Redmire linears, proof enough for me. Sometimes being not quite right in the head pays off. I found the best way to tie the swan shots on to the braid would be with a five turn grinner using dental floss or offcuts of your Black Spider (see diagram) not only does the shot simply slide off the tail of the grinner should you become entangled in a branch or lily pad but if you put the shot directly on the braid, it could cut you off like a knife. So the whole idea was based like any rig I have worked on safety first. Be honest . . . how many of you out there who used a split shot as a counter weight on a braided hook link lost fish by the shot cutting straight through your hook link whilst playing fish?

Chapter Fourteen

For the Love of Music

For as long as I have had a passion for fishing I have had a passion for music, and to write a book about my time spent fishing without mentioning the time spent singing just wouldn't be right! Many well known carp anglers I know are into their music. I have been singing since the age of ten and that is pretty much about the time I started fishing. I grew up on a council estate on Bromley Common as part of a single parent family. I never knew my father and to this day have no idea who he was, nor do I care. My family used to live in Brixton, South London but had moved to Bromley after the war. I have no idea who got me into singing but I do know that most of my aunties played the piano to a really good standard. Don't ask me how or why, but my first gig was singing for the Holy Trinity Church Choir on Bromley Common. Ironically it was dead opposite Oakley Road, which is the road that leads to Keston Fishponds. I used to sing for the choir on wedding days and christenings and some Sunday services and I think my pay back then was half-a-crown for a service and seven shillings and sixpence for a wedding. This gave me a bit of pocket money to squander on sweets. Obviously, like most kids, I was into the sounds of the sixties, The Beatles, The Kinks, The Dave Clarke Five, Herman's Hermits, Manfred Mann, The Small Faces and The Who. My first single I bought was *'The Hippy Hippy Shake'* by the Swinging Blue Jeans. In those days most people were either into the Beatles or The Rolling Stones but I never really got into the Stones. Back then, as now, I have always felt that they were grossly overrated and have been living off a back catalogue of songs for thirty years without writing any new stuff. Jagger's a great entertainer but hardly what you would call a singer! I can remember listening to my record collection in the front room with all the vinyl singles stacked up on the record player and dropping down one after another as they finished playing, and singing along to the songs using a hairbrush as a microphone.

I have no real memory of it but I stumbled into my first band in 1970, a band called Orion. Once again, ironically, we rehearsed up at Keston in the village hall, and then later in Sydenham High Street in an old church. The acoustics were unbelievable. Our first gig was at the Spitfire Club in Biggin Hill and I have to say I shat myself. I was so nervous I can remember hanging on to my microphone stand for dear life and for the whole one and a half hours we played. Although I wished the floor had opened up and swallowed me. there was this other feeling in the pit of my stomach that said, "I like this feeling. I like it a lot." I kind of stumbled through the seventies as most people did - it was a time of experiment and excesses and being part of a rock band playing on the London circuit kind of pushed my

I'm in the white shirt, my first band Orion in 1970

fishing into the background. I don't have many regrets in life but the odd missed opportunity still burns in my soul. It either involved women or music, and one opportunity I missed was of my own doing. An old mate of mine from school had gone to work at a record company and one of my all time favourite bands were The Faces with Rod Stewart on vocals. In my book very few bands could match them for entertainment and my mate had got two tickets for free and back stage passes. If that wasn't enough, he was invited to the after show party back at their hotel. My mate said to come with hom and we would have an outrageous time. There would be drink, drugs and crumpet everywhere! The show was at the Lewisham Odeon. Do you know what, I blew it! At the time I was engaged to a girl called Carol, who I eventually married, even though it only lasted six months. What did I do? Because there was only one spare ticket and I couldn't take her I did the honourable thing and didn't go. What an absolute one hundred percent plank! I bumped into my mate a few days later and he said he had the time of his life! He ended up after a spell-binding show by the Faces by going back to their hotel to an outrageous party where he ended up drinking with Rod, the two Ronnies, Kenney, and Ian Mac. I know it sounds shallow, but I have never felt so gutted in my life, honestly. To this

Heartstealer. . .1980s

day it burns in my soul that I missed a once in a lifetime experience, even more so as THE FACES split up about a year or so later, gutted.

The only other band I saw that were incredible was The Who. I saw them at Charlton Football ground in 1976 .Keith Moon was indeed as mad as a box of frogs. It had been pouring with rain and as The Who ran on stage they all fell over one after the other as the front of the stage was covered in water. Roger Daltrey took off his shammy leather top and started to mop up the water from the stage, as Moony stood up on his tom toms with his hands on his hips and shouted out . . . "That's it Daltrey, mop up the stage, you're nothing but a scrubber!" Every one was in fits of laughter as they launched into 'Won't Get Fooled Again' . . . What a show! That was the first time I had seen lasers used in a show - outstanding.... I stumbled through the seventies playing in a band called Muvvers Ruin. We were signed to a guy called Raleigh St George Lofton, (yeah, I know!) and we were under the watchful eye of a record producer called Chris Warren who also worked for A & M Records. I even went to the Surrey Sound Studios to record a single called Telephone Call. It was there that I got my first taste of what bullshit the music business has to offer. I was told exactly what I had to say, given a biog sheet of what I was supposed to be,

The Grasshopper, Westerham in the late 80s audience

Giving it large to a packed audience

where I came from and what I was like, which was nowhere even close to the truth. It might have been somewhat foolish but I told them to stick their contract right up where the sun doesn't shine. I have absolutely no regrets about that missed opportunity whatsoever. Muvvers Ruin imploded after that, far too many drugs and far too much bullshit. I had made four fantastic mates out of it though, Ronnie Mellor, Sebs, Dave Arkle and Norman Dowley. Sadly Ronnie went on to become a speed freak (who didn't) but then became a heroin addict. It was so sad, that man was one of the funniest geezers I've ever known. I have so many memories of rolling on the floor laughing until my sides hurt. He was a constant source of entertainment. The last time I saw him his face and eyes had turned yellow from the heroin abuse, f***, he was a mess. If ever you needed proof that drugs don't work, he was a prime example. Eventually he moved away from Bromley down to Brighton to try and clean up his act, which to his credit he did. He had got completely clean, but ironically some time later he got into a punch up and was stabbed to death by a heroin addict. As they say, you live by the sword and you die by it. During the mid seventies I had a short spell in a band called Grabba that was a kind of middle of the road rock band with commercial songs. The band secured a publishing deal and started to record songs for an album, but it wasn't really me so I kind of eased my way out of it. This was much to the disappointment of the other guys in the band, but I just cant get into something I don't believe in. Again I had made lifelong friends of the guys in the band, Nigel Hinds, Tony Redmond and Wiggy the drummer. Sadly Tony died of MS, or the effects of it, about four years ago. That is an absolutely terrible disease and when I saw him about two months before he died, he was a shadow of himself - terrible. Nigel topped himself about three years ago now. He had spent his whole life writing songs locked away in his Forest Hill basement flat with the sad misconception that he was going to one day make it big. That day never came, although he had been credited with playing on one of Beverly Craven's albums but that was it. I guess he just woke up one day and realised that it was not going to happen so he couldn't go on and topped himself. What a waste. He had more song writing talent in his little finger than these clowns you see on reality shows and pop contests, but that's not how it works, is it? Take Cheryl Cole for instance, she can't even mime in tune, let alone sing, but she has made a fortune from not being able to sing. But isn't that the way of it these days - it's the standing joke in the music business . . . You look awful, you sound awful, you cant sing in tune but you will make a fortune! Ha, ha, crazy! By the late seventies I had joined a band called Heartstealer, a great bunch of South Londoners who really were at the top of their game, Colin (Woody) Wood, Steve Sinclair, Tony

Redmond and Paul Taff. We did at some point have an Australian guy called Kim on bass and an outstanding lead guitarist called Alex, a Scotsman. We played just about everywhere on the London circuit, Dingwalls, The Rock Garden, Ronnie Scott's, The Music Machine. We ended up playing on the same circuit as Japan, Squeeze, and Nine Below Zero (or Stan's Blues Band as they were known then). One night we were booked to play at the end of tour party for Squeeze, who had been out in the States. It was at a club in Rotherhithe that backed on to the Thames and had a huge wall of thick glass which gave you a fantastic view over the river at night. All I can remember from that night was being joined on stage by some of the guys from The UK Subs and Squeeze, who got up for a jam but I was lured off the stage halfway through a song by a mini skirted hottie and ended up in the back alley with a bottle of wine and a very well known page three girl. Those really were the days I can tell you.

Eventually after a couple of decades Heartstealer split up and I found myself trying to write songs without a band. At the time I was doing marble work and ended up laying a marble floor for Graham Lyle who used to be in McGuinness Flint and Gallagher and Lyle, excellent writers of hit songs. He lives in Bromley. I can remember Graham playing me some tracks he had written for Tina Turner in his recording studio upstairs in the house. I can't remember the exact tracks but they may have been: 'Another Hero', 'Simply the Best', and maybe 'Steamy Windows'. He played me three tracks, which sounded great, and the advice he gave me was if you want a hit record, write something that flows right the way through the song. Obviously I never took his advice! Therefore never wrote a hit record. I got out of music for about six years or so and apart from singing in the Carp Society's Super Group I did very little else. About eight years ago I saw a band in my local called The Ronnies. A bunch of nice guys playing Rod and The Faces stuff and Small Faces with some Stones stuff thrown in and a few Ronnie Lane songs. I loved what they were doing but they didn't have a lead singer, so I went up to them after the gig and said to the rhythm guitarist, "Great set mate, great sound, and you all look fantastic, but you need a lead singer!" He looked at me and I knew he was thinking, "You cheeky bastard," but I gave him a CD with me singing on it and it just happened to have me singing a version of *Stay With Me* by The Faces on it. A week later I got a call asking me to do a gig with them and I sang three or four numbers with them and I've been with them ever since. It is a complete show, good music, we look good and sound good and above all we entertain. We have done the Rod Stewart convention twice up in Blackpool, where we met Rod's lovely sister Mary, an absolute diamond who works her socks off for the cancer charity event. She hosts the

Rod Stewart's sister Mary. What a lovely lady!

The Ronnies at the Rod Convention, Blackpool

weekend event and the auction of Rod's old stage gear, gold discs etc. All proceeds go to the cancer charity. We even had Rod's mandolin/violin player Jana Jacoby get up on stage with us to do some songs - that was really special, thanks Jana. The weirdest thing was when Rod's sister Mary turned up one night with a bunch of friends in a mini bus. We were playing in a wine bar in Coulsdon in Surrey and they just pulled up outside and strolled in, said hello and watched the show. The only thing I can't get round my head is that why would you go and watch a band playing Rod/Faces songs when your brother is Rod Stewart? I do know that Mary likes the band though; maybe it is because we are a bit cheeky and try our best to put on a show and entertain the punters. Another close encounter came when I got an email from Kenney Jones' wife, Jayne, asking if we would play at the Itchycoo Park Festival. The Small Faces and Faces had been inducted into the Rock and Roll Hall of Fame and to celebrate Kenney Jones was going to put on a two day festival organized by his wife Jayne and her associates at their polo club, Hurtwood Park in Surrey. We were booked to play on the Sunday as the second to last act. There were to be loads of well known bands and singers performing all on the same bill, the weather turned rubbish and May was a washout. Three weeks of rain had waterlogged the pitch area where the concert was due to be staged so they cancelled it in case they ruined the pitch. All the big trucks that carry the stage, lighting, rigs and sound system would have torn up the area that would have meant wrecking the polo season for them. Gutted wasn't the word. Hopefully they are going to do it next year and we will be included. At the moment I am also singing in an unplugged type setup that basically is called Ace Faces. Its four lead singers who are from different bands: you have Tony Pepper on acoustic guitar and vocals, Leigh Highwood on piano and vocals, Steve Crispe on acoustic Guitar and vocals and myself on lead vocals and percussion. Basically you get perfect harmonies from four voices and an entertaining show with a great choice of material. I am hoping to write an album with them very soon and actually I am feeling the most comfortable in my singing these days as the unplugged thing is far more rewarding musically and just different to the full on rock band thing. The Ronnies did record a four track EP on which I wrote one track and wrote the lyrics for two of the other songs. I felt it lacked conviction and could have been so much better if it had been produced by a proper producer as opposed to a couple of the boys in the band. Cost is everything in production but it was OK. What the future holds I don't know but I am at the most confident I have ever been in terms of my singing. I think my only discontent with the music business nowadays is the state of it. You have people making records that really shouldn't - most of them just can't sing and they need voice modulators and

Jana Jacoby Rod's violin/mandolin player joined us on stage

Rockin' out with Lee Jackson on bass

auto tuning to even stand a chance of getting it anywhere near right. Backing tracks to help them sound better. It's just awful, all these talentless puppets who can't even mime in tune, you know who I mean . . . It's a bit stale and disappointing really. In my generation people or bands went out and learned their craft first by playing live for a few years then got a record deal.Now they get a deal and try to learn to sing and perform live and that is why the majority sound so poor during live shows. They just can't cut it without backing tapes, voice modulators and auto tune. There is so much talent out on the live circuits it's sacrilege that they don't get an opportunity to move foreward. I went on the X Factor like an idiot and soon realised that it's a reality show not a singing contest. I went up to the new Arsenal ground for auditions and there were some incredible singers there but I was shocked that all the best singers were told they were not wanted. All the talentless ones were given tickets to go to the live shows - quite clearly it is someone's idea of entertainment that decides who goes through not based on singing talent. I don't know how long it's been running but apart from Leona Lewis, try and name a winner who is still around and releases records? Exactly! Personally I think that Simon Cowell should be stood up against a wall and shot for the way he has ruined popular music. The acoustic unplugged thing is gaining popularity and we are starting to spread out into Kent. Hamish, one of the guys from the Average White Band, has a pub down that way and appreciates good music and has booked The Ronnies in the past, and is booking us now. The Hop Festival in Faversham is a hotbed of very good talent, so much better than the rubbish you see on TV. Also it's funny that all the famous people I have come across from the music business are really nice, down to earth, regular people. Maybe that's because they have nothing to prove and they all come from an era where they had to work hard for their success and served their time before they managed to secure a record deal. Sadly the music business is run by corporate companies now, and most of the independent labels have vanished. Labels like Stiff Records that gave individuals the chance to get their talent across and backed them to the hilt. I came so close to securing a record deal and on reflection it's probably for the best that I didn't succeed as I have my doubts as to whether I would still be around to tell the tale. With all the temptations that the music business has to offer I might just have gone off the deep end! Whatever the future holds I will still enjoying getting up in the company of good musicians and entertaining the crowds. I would have to say that there is nothing quite like it, I thrive on the adrenalin, and I love the banter with the audience. It has to be said that singing on stage is the exact opposite to carp fishing and probably why I enjoy both so much, one is full on, and the other is the ultimate in relaxation and escapism! Long may it continue . . .

Lightning Source UK Ltd.
Milton Keynes UK
UKOW06f0615271113

221920UK00001B/1/P